his name was

JACK

Jack J. Galloway 1919-1987

A Sandhills Cowboy

Edited by Nancy J. Galloway Hamar

iUniverse, Inc.
Bloomington

His Name Was Jack
A Sandhills Cowboy

iUniverse books may be ordered through booksellers or by contacting:

iUniverse
1663 Liberty Drive
Bloomington, IN 47403
www.iuniverse.com
1-800-Authors (1-800-288-4677)

ISBN: 978-1-4620-3729-2 (sc)
ISBN: 978-1-4620-3730-8 (e)

Printed in the United States of America

iUniverse rev. date: 8/11/2011

Written for Jack and all those who followed

Contents

FOREWORD

Jack Galloway died in 1987, a year after his mother and two years after his wife, Alice.

When Alice, my mother, died in 1985, he wasn't sure what he'd do without her. I said, "Write. Write a book." Of course, that suggestion was dismissed when he said he was no writer.

In 2005 I wrote about an impending book in my "Up Close" column for a local newspaper. I told my readers my dad was a writer. He had written me letters through the years because I lived 500 miles away from him and Mom. I knew he could write. So I told him to write about each of the horses in his life. I rattled a few off, "Write about Patty Ann, Old Pal, Eagle, Darky and Spike or Harding," I said. "Then write about the people you've known. There was Old Poke Kidder and Floyd Jones, to name a couple."

He was a little slow getting started but he did write me letters about his growing up in the Sandhills of Nebraska. He wrote about his dad getting bucked off when he accidentally goosed Trix with a garden spade. He did not write one about going with his dad when he was just a boy and trailing remount horses from the ranch up to the stockyards at Nenzel or Cody to send them on the train to Fort Robinson at Crawford to the U.S. Cavalry. He wrote over 20 of those stories.

From 1987 to 2010 is a long time but I was working and couldn't spare the time to sit with the letters. I kept them in the safe deposit box because they were precious to me.

There are only three people left on earth who can read his writing. That's my daughter, my sister and me. We hashed around getting the stories typed, organized and printed. My sister's boys and my children knew Granddad Jack. The great-grandchildren did not, but maybe these stories will give them an inkling of the cowboy he was.

I even have a few pictures that could go in a book and I have poetry that Dad wrote. I know of a publisher who prints books like we want to put together. I even have a proofreader ready to go. Only one big thing held me back – I had no computer at home. I had no intention of getting started on the project until the sister gave me that darn computer and even then I protested that I use a Mac at work and I know nothing about other computers. She dismissed that idea with a wave of her hand, saying I'd get used to this one.

There's a part of me that wanted to get right to it. I want to re-read those stories and re-live the times when Dad told them to us. I want to remember Butterfly and the time he saw my mother riding her across the swamp by the river. He was scared but the two of them came right across.

I want to re-read the story about the time a good team of horses kept the buggy upright and got my grandmother, an aunt and several small children across an early springtime river when the ice was breaking up. I want to get reacquainted with the team that hauled a big load of hay down a steep hill from on top of the canyons to the river bottom and didn't spill the hayrack.

Perhaps I should write one story of my own. We lived in a cabin on the Niobrara River bottom and I had a big yard and a dog to play with. I was just a toddler past two but I could talk up a storm. One day my mother realized I was gone. I had been playing with my dad's spurs and she could see the squiggles of the spur rowels in the sand on the road down toward the river.

She could not see me but she would call the dog and he would answer. Then he'd run just far enough for her to see him and return to the river. I'm sure she was imagining her baby floating face down in the water as she tried to reach me.

Mom rounded the bend to the crossing where we usually entered the river and there I was with the dog, still heading east on the path. She asked me where I was going and she said I looked up innocently and said, "I'm taking Daddy his spurs."

My parents always said that dog, called Pup, was part coyote. Later he left the ranch and Dad saw him in a pack of coyotes several times.

This was my story but it shows I knew a cowboy needed his spurs and I knew my dad was a cowboy. The stories in the lock box are Dad's stories.

One memory of my dad was the ride he gave me on my sled. He tied a throw rope to the handles and dallied it on his saddle horn. Then he pulled me around the big yard between the house and the barn. I hung on to the side of the sled for dear life as snow from the horse's feet flew back in my face. He thought it was great fun and I never told him any different. I can feel the snow yet.

Another is a poignant moment as I saw Dad standing on a little knoll in the big yard just before dark. He heard the birds and looked up at the ducks honking their way south high above the ranch buildings. Silently he watched them with a kind of sadness about him. I've never forgotten how he looked standing there.

Thanks to my daughter and sister who have urged me into gear. We will get Jack's book together.

First and foremost, Jack was a cowboy who respected and loved his horses. From his first memory of Trix until Bitsy went down the road, his world revolved around a lifetime with horses. His loneliest times were after we left the ranch in 1948 and he was without a horse. His happiest times were when he was surrounded by them.

He was a trainer ahead of his time as he always told us a horse that was afraid of you will hurt you. A horse that trusts you won't. Jack knew more about the mind and feelings of a horse than most people do, even the so called "experts." He could build equipment for a horse and he could repair all the tack his grandkids could tear up. He even built a horse once. He made two stick horses with wooden heads, leather bridles and even bits for their mouths. No two little girls were better mounted. At a time in our lives when we didn't have a living, breathing horse with us, he built a substitute.

We were living in town once when he decided he would rope us off my bicycle. We ran down the street and he pedaled along behind us, raised up and leaned out to throw a loop. Bicycles don't lean well and his "rope horse" dumped him. As I recall, he was skinned up considerably. That was the last time he tried bicycle roping.

In his own way, Jack believed in a Creator. He knew somebody was responsible for the changing of the seasons, someone who made the grass green up one last spring for an old cowboy.

May he rest in peace. Please let him join Alice and please, Lord, let him breath free again and let horses run in grass clear up to their knees in his heaven.

Now fast forward to today and you are holding a collection of Jack Galloway's stories and poems in your hand. Putting this together is a tribute to the man who was one of the last of his generation of Sandhills cowboys.

He was a personable man who could ride a horse, rope, sing, dance and, unknown to him, he could write. Enjoy his stories.

Nancy Galloway Hamar

A special thanks to Becky Hamar Nickols for her support, technical expertise and deep love for her Granddad Jack Without her help the book would not have been completed in a timely manner.

Thank you to Martin Bergin for graciously allowing us to use his poem "That Old Saddle" in this book

THE BEGINNING OF THESE STORIES

WELL – HERE I am starting to put on paper some of the things that happened, in the past, on the ranch south of Kilgore. Now as I have decided, this ranch was mainly a horse outfit, breaking horses to ship to Iowa or wherever a market could be found.

They carried a Hambletonian stud most of the time to use on native mares to be used as both saddle and buggy horses. Of course, they had a herd of cattle but I don't remember how many as the horses were the main project.

They did quite a lot of farming and my Dad said they never had a decent team on the place as every time a good horse was well broken, Granddad would ship him to Iowa and they would have to break some more. They had to farm and put up hay with whatever junk was left on the ranch.

However this did not hold true on the saddle stock. Of course they sold some but got to keep the better ones to use at home.

They got in financial trouble in the early '20's, as did a lot of ranches. It wasn't so much the ranch itself but the insurance company that held the paper on the place went broke and as Dad said, "They couldn't run fast enough to find $2.50 an acre to refinance."

They closed up about 1925. My Uncle took a bunch of work horses to Scottsbluff, Nebr. and put in a lot of the original irrigation ditches for the sugar beet fields.

I was pretty small but Mom, Dad, and I drove there with a Model T Ford. I remember standing at one end of the tunnel that is under the "Wild Cat" hills and they used little mules to pull the dirt out of the tunnel. They had a cook wagon where my aunt did the cooking and fed the men. We slept in a tent at night. Even though I was small I'm sure they unhooked an awful lot of horses in the evenings and the equipment covered a lot of ground. We were just there for a visit and it seemed to be a long long way home.

The next year my Dad, both Granddads and some uncles built the house, barn, and grainery on the school section where the rest of this story took place. One day my Mom and I were coming back to the old ranch from the new house. Got caught in a hail storm. We were horseback and crawled in a brush patch and held our horses. There was a lot of hail but it wasn't very big. When we got home I still had hail stones in my hair. I have always insisted when I don't think right that my brain was frozen.

Now this school section wasn't even fenced. There was a little pasture with a fence around it and all livestock had to be put there until the boundary could be fenced. In fact, the little house out back hadn't been built yet but fortunately, the brush grew close to the house.

Dad had bought some old buildings a mile or so north of our place and hauled one in from there. From that time on our life revolved around building fence. That's a big job when you think of fencing a house yard, hog pasture, boundary fence and corrals, also garden. As this had to be done between some farming, gardening and everything that goes with everyday living, our lives were built around putting in fence.

Granddad Galloway built a rock cellar and it was our pride and joy. Gave us a pleasant and safe place to go if a bad storm seemed to be in the making. We never had a storm where it was needed but we would sit by the door and watch the clouds pile up. The dogs, cats and people would all gather there. I always felt so safe and when the rain came we would run for the house and get wet on the way. Mom always put her apron over whatever little one was small. It was usually late afternoon or evening so everything stopped for supper.

That old cellar was sure an important part of life. You lived out of it most of the year. Didn't go to town too often and even though my folks bought a few things more than some people, our living was in the cellar. Of course, there was no refrigerator so in warm weather all the meat was canned and put there. Grocery list was mainly important staples liked flour, kerosene, sugar and of course tobacco.

Always had a bunch of setting hens in the spring. How I remember waiting for those baby chicks getting large enough to fry. We were never hungry. We raised a big garden and Dad was a good gardener. That, so with chickens, a few hogs for lard and canned meat we got along fine even through hard times in the 30's.

Also, before I forget, our getting along all hinged on a bunch of milk cows. I swear I have spent more time wrangling milk cows than any other thing else. You milked in the morning before you went to work. You milked before you went to bed. You milked before you went out at night and you milked when you got home. It was the only steady money anyone had. My Dad always milked 8. He said 7 wasn't enough and 9 was too many for one man to milk. I never knew how he figured it out but it did work.

We had a couple of bob tailed cows and I swear I still have bumps on my head from being pounded in the summer when the flies were bad. One time when my brother Don was small one of these cows hit him on the head. He stood up and kicked her in the belly. That cow had a long tail and it wrapped around his feet. His shoes had hooks on them where they laced up and her tail hung up in them. Of course he came unhooked but he was a pretty dirty kid when he came loose.

Had a hired man once. He walked in during the hard times about '30 or '31. He worked for awhile for his room and board and was glad to get it. Dad paid him at haying and corn picking four cents a bushel. Dad always said he was the best man he ever had as he would be up in the morning before everyone else and go milk. He wasn't worth a darn for anything else and I wanted Dad to fire him. He thought a minute and agreed the guy wasn't much good but look how many more cows we would have to milk if he wasn't there. Needless to say, I got along real well with the hired man after that.

Times were tough in the '30's. No jobs except haying and corn picking.

A steady job paid 10 to 15 bucks a month if you could get one. I got 5 cents a bushel picking corn in '38 and times were getting better then. That Sandhill corn would run about 12 to maybe 20 bushels per acre. I could almost pick $2 worth a day and thought I was getting rich.

Have strayed away from what I intended to write so will start over.

Intended to write about horses or at least some of them that I have been with through the years. As everyone knows, everything revolved around horses when I was born in 1919. Can well remember going to town with team and buggy as we didn't get a Model T till about '24. Will just throw these stories out and sort them later. Speaking of buggies, my Dad took me with him to go pick a mess of June berries. I was about four. One mare was named Topsy. I guess he got the berries picked and we started home. We were going down a steep part of Cottonwood Hill when something either broke or she wasn't hooked tight enough. The buggy touched her rear end, she snorted, and started to kick. Now, the dashboard on a buggy isn't very far from your feet and very close to the horses. When the storm cleared we were all right but the dash was sure gone from the buggy. That's the last I remember the mare so I guess Uncle Charley took her to Scottsbluff.

That Cottonwood Hill was a thorn in the flesh of the public. Of course, when the cars first came out there it was just a buggy road. If a Model T was working absolutely perfect it could just make it over. If it didn't make it over they would stop. Everyone got out and the car backed down the hill. Then the driver would take as good a run as they could. When they got to the place where the people were standing everyone, women, kids, and men, would push. That usually was enough help to get on up. Then the car would stop, everyone walked up the hill and loaded up again.

None of the fences had car crossings in them at that time so everyone tried to take a man along to open gates. That's how most women and kids learned to drive. They would drive through the gates as the man opened and closed them. You didn't rate a trip by miles. You rated by the number of gates.

This hill was on the old ranch and when we got the first car there was just Mom, Dad, and me. Dad would ride a saddle horse to the hill and Mom would drive. Dad would put his rope on the car and take off in high gear. At the top of the hill, and we always made it, he would tie the horse and pick him up on the way home.

I would never try to tell anyone how much I know or have taught horses. I can write for a long time what horses have taught me.

I can't remember when I didn't have my own horses and saddle. The only trouble with that was I thought I was 20 years old and a finished cowboy. My Dad took me with him all the time if it was possible. I can remember yelling my head off and shedding buckets of tears if I couldn't go with him or the trip was too long to suit him.

He must have been a darn good teacher, and I know he was, or I would never have lived to grow up. I will try to get some of his teachings in here because some of his training must have got me out of trouble because if I was horseback I had no fear of God, man, or the devil himself. On the ground I was or felt pretty meek and mild.

Some of this can be attributed to my first horse. At least I claimed him and there was a sure enough fight if anyone tried to borrow him. His name was Trix and probably the most foolproof horse ever born. He was born and raised there on the ranch. I don't know who broke him but my Dad and Uncle Charley finished him and he was always with us. My first memory of being horseback was on him and I was too small by far to ride alone. I remember leading him around and I suppose I thought he was a dog. However, old Trix was capable of getting his point across very quick if something didn't suit him. You could crawl over, under, hang on his tail and sleep under him and though he was never asleep he would not and never did step on me.

However, in the spring if he wasn't used and got fat and sassy he would buck and he knew how. A pretty good cowboy would have to ride him for a week and he was alright. Probably wouldn't have bucked with a girl or little kid because he had a lot of feelings but that's the way they worked it.

You absolutely could *not* tie him up. In the barn he would stay tied with a piece of twine but outside he would pull back every time. Of course he was smart enough not to pull but once on a heavy halter or chain. He would stay close anywhere you turned him loose but tied up was a no-no. That's one of the first things he taught me was don't tie me up. Of course, we tore the railing off the porch. A whole bunch of bridles and a hay rack or two before I learned.

Probably my Dad's threats helped some also as that was the worst thing he threatened me with was, behave or I'll turn your horse loose. Believe me, I shaped up in a hurry. My Dad never hit me in my life but the threat of no horse was enough. Pure hell on a five year old cowboy to be set afoot. He only had to do it once. Then he relented and gave me an ear of corn to catch Trix with. He never had to repeat the lesson.

You could put as many kids on him as could get up there but once in a while if the person behind the saddle was a little heavy he would get indignant.

I was less than three and Dad put me in the saddle and got on behind. Mom handed him a shovel and some watermelon seeds. Trix was pretty young at the time. We went a couple of hundred yards and I guess Trix decided to put a stop to what to him was foolishness. He stared to buck and me, the shovel, and seeds was too much for Dad to hold onto so he bailed out. Lost his balance and came down on both hip pockets behind me. I was still on and can still see Dad sitting there on the ground. I think he had broken his ribs before and was hurting too bad to get up. Anyway, Trix and I waited till the storm cleared and I had learned if you rode Trix double be very very sure to do it gently.

Another time Dad turned his work horses loose. It was evening and the horses started to go to pasture. Dad told me not to follow them but as usual, I didn't listen. We got about a quarter of a mile from the barn and I decided to come back. Trix proved he was bigger than me. He stopped and stayed there but I couldn't get him to turn around and come back as he thought he should go along, I gave up and got off to lead him back. I suppose I was about five at the time. An old cow had a calf by the trail. When I came walking by she let out a beller and took a run at me. Luckily she spooked old Trix and I was between his front legs. Every time I started to come out of my safe place she would take another run at us. I was yelling and bawling so loud they heard me at the house and came to the rescue.

Right there I learned from Trix – Don't follow the work horses off and never get unmounted if you can help it.

About this same time Dad dealt for a bay horse at Kilgore. He was supposed to be a kid horse and I guess he probably was but he wasn't Trix. They were a little short on saddle horses and wanted Trix in the saddle string. I didn't think too much of the project, but as I still had the bay horse, we called Ginger, didn't fuss too much.

Dad was riding for the Davidson outfit who had cattle on the Forest Reserve and left each morning to go ride hills and pastures. About a half mile west of our buildings there was a gate. I always wanted to ride to the gate with Dad and then come home. He always let me go after I promised not to lope on the way back home. Every time I tried to lope back that damn horse would duck into a cow trail and set me afoot. I would start to yell and bawl, Dad would hear me and come back, give me the devil, remind me I wasn't supposed to lope, get me mounted, and go on to work.

Dad said later that he thought I would eventually get tired of falling off and stop loping the horse but that I never did. Each day I would think I would finally make it but never did. Although it was another horse I learned another lesson that concerned Trix. I let him get away, so I always knew after that to never never let anyone get away with your top horse.

A Poem for Alice - Life on the River

You said write you a poem
To leave to all our kids
About them long long years ago
And about the things we did.

So here's some of it they won't believe
There's any reason to it
But I'll get it down as best I can
And you just start sortin' through it.

Can you recall the time at all?
You were brought out on the river
To meet all your future in laws
God it must have made you shivver.

Now we all knew that you were apt
To give married life a whirl
We were warned that you weren't beautiful
But you sure were a damn good girl.

You girls settled in
You did just what you could
It was dishes, kid and diapers
You were doing what you should.

Of all the things we put you through
It's a wonder you survived
So many things we didn't have
Yes, it's a wonder you survived

You came from town and the horse fell down
In the cold and icy river
It happened of course there were 4 on the horse
God I think of it and shiver.

There were rattlesnakes and the damn roof leaked
Nobody had a car
If you left home of course you took a horse
So you didn't go too far.

Remember the time we crawled the hill
To roll up the glass in the car
Just a kerosene light that stormy old night
No sign of the moon or a star.

And my dirty white hound came up from behind
And stuck his cold nose on my rump
I'll sure guarantee there was just you and me
Inside of that car in one jump.

Remember the time you took Clementine
On a night that was dark as all Hades
Hung a gas lamp on the front to sort out the bumps
And took off like a brand new Mercedes.

***Clementine was a 1929 Plymouth they had. She was always referred to
as "she" and she even had a rumble seat.

Jack and Alice

GINGER

JUST A QUICK THING that don't concern Pal but was a stunt I pulled by not doing what I was told.

The horse was Ginger that I mentioned dumping me in the brush because I insisted on loping home.

I was four or five and I think someone was to use Ginger on this particular day. Anyway, he had a saddle on him that wasn't mine. I knew Ginger was supposed to be my horse so I insisted they let me lead him around in the house yard until they were ready to leave.

It was pretty early in the morning and it probably wasn't long until I got bored leading him around while he grazed. It seemed like the men were a little slow getting ready to leave than I expected and I turned Ginger loose and went to the house. I was standing on that big porch when he grazed under Mother's four wire clothesline. The wires were exactly the same height as the saddle horn and he went under almost in the middle.

I'll guarantee the stuff hit the fan when he came out the other side. All four wires were hung around the horn. Behind that came posts and guy wires. He bucked clear across the yard and hit a box corner in a woven wire fence. That turned him around and he came back through the clothes line the second time. By that time he was winded and tangled up so bad he fell and laid there.

The men came from the barn and got him untangled but the horn was jerked out of the saddle and the tree was broke all to hell.

Ginger wasn't hurt, Mom never did get the clothes line back up until we moved to the school section and put it up there. I was a little afraid my rear might be due for a kicking as I stood on the porch and watched them untangle Ginger. They all seemed to be of the same opinion but as usual as long as no one was hurt nothing much more was said to me but I didn't get to lead any more horses in the yard.

Trouble at School

Probably the worst stunt I ever pulled I did on purpose but didn't expect such a complete example of what I only intended to be a funny, ornery stunt.

We had a lady teacher who rode a horse to school. I suppose he was a little goosey and pulled back easy. Anyway, for some reason she always tied this horse in the end stall in the barn. The next stall was left empty so no one needed to bother her horse. She rode with a bridle and halter and always had the halter to tie him up with. We all had orders to stay away from that stall. Of course, after your horses were put in the barn in the morning, going back in before school was out in the afternoon was a no-no anyway.

In a lot of ways this teacher seemed a little mean to us and had beat up a couple of the older boys pretty bad. At least we thought so and in later years I was sure of it. Of course, they couldn't do anything to get even so, as I was small, in fact 8 because it was my first year in the country school. I decided to do it for them and then tell about it later.

School was let out for the afternoon so when we took our horses out of the barn to go home, I carefully forgot my dinner pail by the east barn door. We all rode away and I just happened to remember I had forgotten my dinner pail, which got rid of all the kids.

I tied my horse to the yard fence, slipped in the east barn door, which was seldom used and started sneaking up on the school ma'ms horse. I knew how to let a horse watch you close and then move quick and spook heck out of them.

By the time I had eased and slipped and really had the old horse's attention, he was in a pretty good sweat. Now, all I really intended to do was make him pull back, break loose, and set the teacher afoot so she would have to walk home.

I got to the empty stall. He had his halter rope good and tight so I

11

figured the time was right to start the ball rolling. I jumped about a foot in the air, waved both arms and yelled "BOOOO!"

I expected some action but nothing like what took place.

I suppose that was as close to a tornado as I ever want to get. He sure enough pulled back. The halter was better than I expected and he brought the manger right along. That gave him enough slack he was headed out the barn door with the halter rope between his front legs and most of the manger on his rump.

He took out the barn door, about one-third of the south side of the barn. Then he had enough slack to really go into action. Now this horse had a squeal and it was stuck in high C. I have heard horses who were scared or mad squeal but usually they stop after three or four times.

This old boy's squealer never let up. Of course the school ma'm heard the racket start and stepped out of the door just in time to see a squealin' cyclone with part of a barn tied to him coming straight at her. Needless to say, that put her back inside with the door shut just as he went past.

By the time he kicked, bucked, and squealed his way around the schoolhouse he was back to the school yard gate. He was still tied to a pretty good chunk of a 2 x 6 that was hitting his rump about every third jump. When he went over the hill out of my sight, he was still running, still squealing and still getting whomped with the 2 x 6.

The teacher not only walked home, she walked to and from school the rest of the year. When she came out of the schoolhouse I was riding very carefully away. She wanted to know what happened and I very carefully admitted forgetting my dinner bucket and when I stopped in to get it, I guess it spooked her horse.

Fortunately for me, the horse was considered sort of a screwball and given to dingy stunts.

Outside of the barn having to be nearly rebuilt, nothing more was ever mentioned. And believe me, this is the only time I ever admitted exactly how the school ma'ms horse got loose.

Jack and Wildcat

When I Get My Revenge

Today I was late,
I have to stay in,
Because I poked Nell
In the back with a pin.

It wasn't my fault,
She sat straight in her desk,
My hand just slipped out
And you know the rest.

Nell gave a yelp,
The teacher came back,
She asked Nell who poked her,
And Nellie said, "Jack."

The teacher looked at me,
With blood in her eye.
She says you'll stay in
'Till a quarter of five.

It doesn't seem right,
So I'm asking you,
Should a fella stay in
For what his hands do?

The clock's gone around,
It's a quarter past four,
I have to stay in
For a half an hour more.

When I get to heaven,
St. Peter I'll tell
To send that old teacher
Back down to hell.

Then I'll float around,
In my white gauzy wings,
I'll laugh and I'll dance
While a shovel she swings.

Yes I'm going to have fun.
I very well know,
When I'm up in heaven,
And teacher's below.
In all my solitude,
Jack Galloway

ORNERY KID

BY NOW YOU MIGHT have the idea that I was just an ornery little kid. You would be right up to a point. My Dad was not a hitter, or a paddler, he was a yeller. He yelled if you forgot to be as good as you could be. He yelled if you were naughty. As you grew older you could tell by the sound of his yell what the immediate future was going to be.

He never hit me in my life but he had more ways to make me behave than I thought possible. When I was small he would threaten to turn my horse loose. Being separated from old Trix was a fate worse than death when you are four years old.

He even did it once, then relented and gave me an ear of corn to catch him with. That was the only time he had to do it, I believe. Another time we were rounding up the school section to move the cattle to some corn stalks he had rented five or six miles away. I was older by then and been on a lot of roundups. Figured I had about everything figured out. I probably did and never got in much trouble except with a rope or my mouth.

I took exception to something and said so in no uncertain terms. He told me to get off my horse. No way was I afraid but when he used that tone of voice the better part of valor was to get with it. We were about a quarter of a mile from home and he made me unsaddle and turn my horse loose. Old Wildcat started walking down the road real slow with me behind him. Dad made me come back and carry my saddle home also. He said the saddle wasn't too heavy and by the time I got home I might have decided not to talk back to the boss on a roundup. It was sure a put down lesson but I never had any more trouble on anyone's roundup. He needed me to move the cattle so he brought my horse in with him and I got to go on with the cattle drive.

You could get away with anything once but don't do it again after he told you to stop. I don't know what he would have done but I sure was never interested in finding out either.

One time when I was four we were rounding up what is known as Lloyd Olsen's west end. The old ranch still owned it and had taken George Monnier's cattle to summer. Dad and I rode up there pretty early in the morning and were throwing the cattle out of the hills down on the river bottom to meet some more riders later. We had a good bunch of cattle headed down a long ridge when Dad saw one lone cow across a deep canyon on a ridge. He told me just to follow the cattle on to the river and wait for him there as he was going after the lone cow.

He rode around the head of the canyon where the going was not rough. Got to the cow and it turned out she had lost a calf and left with the other cattle. She still didn't want to leave the calf and Dad was having quite a time getting her started. I was sure he needed some help and it was just exactly what was necessary to take care of the situation. Couldn't have an old man there by himself with a fighting cow. Honestly, that's what I thought.

I didn't know the way around the head of the canyon so I just pointed Trix that direction and held on. Now I can show you that canyon where we had to have crossed. I studied it many times in later years trying to remember where we could have possibly been. I know it must have been possible because Trix and I made it. We got to Dad still fighting the old cow. He looked at me surprised and asked where in hell I came from. I said my cattle were going all right and I could see he was having trouble so I came across the canyon the help him.

He said, "I'll be damned. I don't believe it. Where did you cross that canyon?" I sure couldn't tell him. Just held onto Trix and came across. Just another example of a kid without brains enough to be scared and a horse that took care of them both.

Dad just roped the old cow and we went to the river. On the way Dad put me back behind the cattle I should have stayed with and I had my orders real plain. "By _____ whatever happens you stay there." I didn't need to be told a second time.

The Double U and A Little Boy in Trouble

WILL SLIP IN A couple of items about the use of a "double u" and some horses it was used on. As I have mentioned they didn't break work horses or any others until at least four years or older. Quite often these horses were big, wild, old and mean and a bronc man really needed some help. He got it from the double u harness. It was a good wide leather belt buckled around a horse's belly. To this was fastened a system of rings and pulleys fastened to the horse's front feet and controlled by ropes threaded through and trailing behind the horse.

They would just front foot the bronc, throw them, tie them down and when they let them up they were wearing the double u and helpless if you pulled the ropes from behind. They could walk or run, but just a little tug on the trailing rope and they would fall. I mean a very little tug. This rig was very easy to overuse and often was, but I'll get to that later.

Before we left the old ranch Dad had dealt some unbroke horses to George Hendershot. In the deal he was to help George get them started and they were starting them pretty fast as George needed them to start farming.

They were working on a little grey mare. Had her in a double u with a harness on. I was sitting on the fence watching what I thought was a real fun thing. This mare seemed to want to strike pretty bad. Dad would walk up in front of her and when she struck George would stand her on her head.

They both went to the barn to get old Duke, the bronc horse, intending to hook up and get the first drive out of the way.

I think I was four years old or maybe five years old. I know I wasn't six because that's when we moved to the home ranch and it wasn't that year.

As soon as they were out of sight I jumped down in the corral. I knew I was all right because I could do anything once without getting in too much trouble.

The mare was pretty winded and as she was bridled couldn't see me anyway. I got behind her and popped her with the rope. Of course she jumped and I sat down on the double u just exactly like the big boys did. Only thing was I didn't slack off. I just sat down and held her there. She was bawling, the harness was rattling and I was pulling holding her down. With those double u's it didn't take much pull.

Dad and George came out of the barn on the run. Couldn't see me but I saw them. Thought I might be in trouble but figured when Dad stopped to open the corral gate I would crawl over the south fence. He double crossed me and jumped over the north one. I let the rope go and started to run and scramble. That fence seemed about twenty feet high before I came to the top and when I got there just stood up and jumped. I took off for the house on a dead run with Dad yelling that if I came back again that day he would do something like cut my ears off.

As anyone knows, he could have caught me, but I never went back that day nor did I ever hold another horse down with a double u.

Horse Roundup

I<small>T WAS THE LAST</small> big horse roundup held on the Forest. As I have
mentioned before, everyone used it for fall grazing and dumping grounds
for horses not in use at home.

The XU had leased all of the Forest so the powers that be declared a
horse roundup on all pastures and told everyone to show up and get their
horses on a certain day at Sanford's corral. All of the outlying pastures had
been rounded up and thrown into the Galloway division to be corralled on
that day.

Dad had let me ride Penny. He could fair fly and Dad knew I wouldn't
get left behind. There were between three and four hundred head of these
horses and that is quite a sight.

In a big herd like that there are always some horses called bunch quitters.
It may be a fighting stud with several particularly wild mares or possible an
old mean mare with a half dozen of her colts following her. These horses
don't separate regardless how tight the herd is held. How they keep track of
each other in a bunch that large no one can understand but they manage.

When they decide to break out, they just come. They will run around
you, over you, all at the same time; you can't turn them and they just run
off.

They had shot a fighting stud out of the bunch the day before and that
pretty well took care of his mares. They stayed in the bunch.

Dad had told me there was a small bunch he expected to break out. He
told me if it happened and he took them to stay right where he left me and
don't pay attention to anyone.

Sure enough the bunch broke out, Dad took them and Penny and I
stayed put. A rider came by and told me to come along. I said, "No" and I
thought he was going to try to get a hold of Penny and make us go along. It
didn't worry me much because I knew he couldn't get close enough to Penny

to hit him with a thirty foot rope. He went on, they took the big bunch in to the corrals but Penny and I stayed put.

Dad and Old Pal took the bunch quitter two and a half miles west to the end of the pasture. Then two miles south to that fence, then two and a half back east then two miles north again to where he left me. He said at one time he had lost them but followed their tracks for a ways and as they were winded he caught up with them.

It seemed to me he had been gone a week but I was older by then, I was six. I damn well camped there. Finally way off to the south, I could see some dots coming and sure enough old buckskin Pal was on their tails. As they got closer I did ride toward them. Pal was a little winded but Penny had plenty of run in him so Dad slowed down and Penny and I took them to the fence corner. They had all the run they wanted and when Pal got his wind we took them on to the corral with no trouble.

That time I stayed where I belonged.

Tying Hard and Fast vs. Dallying

You hear a lot of pros and cons about when to dally and when to tie hard and fast. Never learned to dally and what few times I needed to I was so interested in keeping all my fingers attached to my hand I usually wound up dropping my rope and having to run the critter down anyway. But I do remember very well where and why I learned to tie hard and fast and to hell with in between.

For some reason our outfit seemed to only own one throw rope at a time. Of course this was long before nylon and such was invented because we never saw those till after WW2. For years I thought those old grass ropes were born with a knot in the middle where someone didn't slack off fast enough. Anyway Dad always let me carry the rope on my saddle and was awful good to let me have a loop or two any time we rode out as long as you were damn careful not to upset any of the stock.

Dad and I were in some brush and came on a pretty lamed up steer. Dad says, "Go ahead and catch him." I built a loop and old Trix and I took off in the heavy brush hot on the old steer's trail. I could hear Dad behind me raising hell about something but Trix and I sure didn't listen 'cause we had a critter to catch. I suppose I was about 5.

Finally Dad cut across some way and got in front of us so we had to stop. By that time Dad had a good head of steam up. I found out in a hurry if you're going to rope something, get tied on that saddle horn 'cause if you're just lucky enough to catch that son-of-a-gun he didn't have any time to hunt me and his rope both up.

Needless to say when we took the next run that old grass rope was hard and fast on my saddle horn. Honestly, that's the last time to this day I ever opened a loop on top of a horse that wasn't there to stay.

That's when I learned if you don't want them, don't rope them. Of course again, I was on old Trix and that's a long ways from some of this junk we have to use now.

Trix had a mate. Another white horse named Penny. Now Penny was just as gentle in his own way as Trix but was terrifically fast. To my knowledge he never was outrun on a road but you absolutely could not race him on a track in a bunch of horses because he simply would run away anywhere but ahead. He moved real sharp and shied a lot. He had been snake bitten as a colt and if anything moved under him he was air borne.

I got to ride him quite a lot but just on very special occasions. I imagine I was about 10 and talked Dad into letting me ride him to school for one day.

Now I had heard the big boys talk about riding home late evenings and roping the neighbors' stock. They were training their horses this way. They had been doing this for a year or so and I knew it but that kind of stuff you kept to yourself. If anyone found out you told you were headed for a new kicking out behind the barn.

So Penny and I were coming home from school and the sun goes down pretty fast after those old rural schools let out. I honestly just happened to get into a bunch of the neighbor's cattle and thought about those guys having roped them. I didn't realize they were front footing the cows so after she was down they just rode up and the rope came off.

In my usual hurry up way I tied hard and fast. That Penny horse could fair go to a cow and he did. I couldn't have missed her on purpose. It was just as simple as roping a post but Penny and I are tied hard and fast to about 1,300 pounds of the maddest cow you ever saw. Of course all the other cattle ran off and there I was.

On Penny I was safe as a cherub in church but that fighting cow kept me up there too. Being tied to big mad cattle was nothing new to Penny but I couldn't get loose. My rope pulled down so tight on my saddle horn I absolutely couldn't untie it. No way was I about to get off so there we were.

After awhile Penny and me had the old cow down and it's a standstill but I sure couldn't go home with 1,300 pounds of the neighbor's beef. I bawled awhile, rested awhile. Finally decided to start chasing the cow home ahead of me. Penny and I could probably have managed it eventually but I have always thought my Dad was a little suspicious of why I wanted Penny just for a day.

Anyway, here came Dad on Old Pal, puffing his corncob pipe. I knew I was in a bad spot but was sure glad to see him. He didn't say a word, just looked the situation over. He was strong enough in his fingers to untie my rope. He kicked the old cow in the rump, loped up beside her and jerked the loop off.

Not too big a job since Penny and I had about broke her to milk anyway. He just coiled up the rope, handed it to me and said, "Guess that will teach you to keep your damned rope on your saddle won't it?" I said "Yes" and to this day it has never been mentioned.

Lessons Learned as a Kid

AT ONE TIME DAD had cleaned up most of the junk horses around the outfit. Traded some old stuff for some corn and others on a break-one-take-one deal. He didn't make much of a point in getting his share back.

There was six or eight broke mares left and one had a stud colt. He intended to get a half a dozen colts and then get rid of everything except the colts. We did get the stud broke to lead and pretty gentle, then turned him out.

One rider if he was pretty well mounted could bring these horses off the forest to the corral but it was a pretty touchy job. One day Dad left to go to the field about five miles away. I wasn't as big as I thought I was, and as I could get away with anything once, I decided to round up these horses and play with them in the corral and get them turned out before Dad got home.

I was riding old Eagle and though he wasn't much for smart, was a hell of a good roundup horse. He was just a plain old bay horse but he inherited me at the time I was beginning to decide I knew more than most anybody about being a cowboy. I suppose I was about eleven or twelve and as no one else used Eagle we sort of came on together. It's a good thing he took good care of me because even though he didn't know much, he still knew more than me.

He was out of an almost full blood Hambletonian mare and Lord only knows what stud. I think Dad gave someone an unbroken workhorse to rough him out. They brought him back about half broke. Dad could ride him all right, but he did buck a couple of times. Dad didn't have time or need for him so he let a guy use him for awhile. He quit bucking but hadn't learned anything when we got him back.

I brought the bunch into the corral with no trouble. Up to that point I probably was just proving old Eagle and I could do it so I could brag a little. Decided to see if the stud was still broke to lead. I caught him and snubbed him to the snubbing post. He raised quite a fuss and was pretty tired when he finally gave up. Then I decided to see what he looked like under a saddle. He threw quite a fit but as he had been broke to be tied up, I finally had him saddled. Decided to go all the way and put my bridle on.

There we were and the fuss had been going on for an hour or maybe a lot more and we were both wringing wet as it was a hot day in the middle of summer.

I stepped back to admire my work, looked around, and there sitting on the corral fence was my Dad. I didn't know what to say I was so surprised and I sure had intended to turn the horses out before he came home.

To this day I don't know how long he had been there. I was a little set for a verbal working over but again I was surprised. He asked, "Is that saddle tight?" I shook it and answered "Yes." He said, "Is that bridle alright?" I looked it over and said "Yes." He said, "Alright let's see what you look like in the middle of that horse."

I knew that I was way past the point of no return and I bet for a moment I was the smallest cowboy who ever set a foot in that corral. I unsnubbed the colt real careful. Stepped up a lot more careful and got away lucky. He just walked out aways and stopped. Dad said, "Alright, now unsaddle and turn them back out and don't you ever saddle another horse on this damn outfit unless you intend to get on."

As the years went by I never forgot and the few times I waited around for a couple of months before I got my nerve up. I never turned one loose after he was saddled.

Trading Pigs with Dad for a Colt

ONE TIME KUDELKA'S, WHO had a truck, came by with a load of pigs they had sold to Joseph's except for one which was a little sow and somewhat bigger but just ready to wean. I guess my dad figured all kids should own one pig and as I had a few bucks in the bank I was immediately in the hog business.

I had to feed her night and morning in the feed way of the barn and she turned into a *very* fat pig and very prolific. Now this sow was mine and it was my job to pen her up and get her out of any trouble she could think of to get into and there was a lot.

We made it O.K. but I noticed she seemed slower, not so anxious to run from me, and a hell of a lot fuller. In fact didn't seem to eat much or want any. Of course I was only 6 years old and though all the farm facts of life were well known to me I never suspected anything like that could happen to my nice little porker pig. But it did and one morning she had 8 pretty little ones in the hay stack.

Just another damn day for me but the hired man wised me up. Seven of my little ones were sows. Only one boar. Now if 7 sows had pigs twice a year I was one rich kid cause I could feed Dad's corn. I admit my arithmetic was used that summer because if I could figure right in a couple of years I could corner the hog market. I'm pretty sure Dad was trying to figure out how to get me out of the business with no hard feelings.

Luckily the Rothleutner outfit had shipped in some Mexican mares in years past. Horses were cheap, there was plenty of range so no one paid too much attention where they ran as the Forest Reserve didn't care either. There were two of these mares who had colts. And that's how Dad got my pigs.

He traded me one colt for a whole pen of hogs and I imagine we were both two of the happiest men on the Niobrara River. Especially him because according to my calculations he got about 10,000 for the 1 colt. Of course he had to feed them cause there my obligations ceased.

Incidentally when this mare grew up she was well broken, Alice rode her when she was pregnant and so was the mare, and they crossed a mud hole that to this day in 1986 that no one will try, but that's a different story.

PUTTING A BELL ON THE WILD COW

HIS DOESN'T GO WITH horses. Just a story of a particular stunt my cousins, the Anderson boys, and I pulled. I think my Uncle Art would have had us all locked up if he could have figured a way to disown us. The Cousins and I were pretty small. I doubt if any of us were over 10. We found an old cow bell somewhere that had lost its clapper and wouldn't ring. I had watched my Dad fix a lot of cowbells as we usually milked about 8 head of cows and had bells on most of them as we all liked to hear them ring as they came in at night.

After the bell was working we found a strap for the cow's neck and had to decide what cow to put it on and how to manage the procedure so as not to get in trouble.

My cousin, Ladd, was real quiet and wasn't addicted to getting into trouble so we sent him up to ask Uncle Art if he could put the bell on a cow. Uncle Art said, without thinking, to go ahead as Ladd didn't need much watching. If me or my cousin Bob had asked him he would have immediately have said no, cause everyone sure knew we needed watching.

I had seen a lot of bells put on new cows and knew what a fit they could throw till they were used to the noise and the leather collar.

Exactly how we kept the cows in the next morning I don't remember. Anyway we had them in a four wire corral when Uncle Art left to go to town. They had one cow who was really a bronc. She could kick, fight, really mean, but could be milked if everyone was careful and nothing happened.

She seemed exactly the cow to wear the bell as far as I was concerned and as there was a snubbing post in the corral where Uncle Art tied the cows he was breaking to milk were all set up. I took my rope, they chased the cow to me and I laid it on dallied the snubbing post and all hell broke loose. She bucked and bawled and tore up a lot of dirt but when things cleared away she was about played out and her head was tight against the post.

We tied on the bell, slipped the rope off and stepped back. Now I had seen a lot of cows go through this but nothing like the fit she threw. She bellered, bawled, bucked, went absolutely nuts, out through the four wire fence on the south side of the corral taking all the rest of the cows along. She tore up the earth for a ways east and came back through another four wire fence and back into the corral through a gate that was closed till she got there.

We managed to put the other cows in the lane so they would go to the pasture but the last we saw of the cow that morning she was backing down the lane still trying to shake off the bell and catch the other cows.

As I recall all we got was a chewing out for the stunt and I'm sure we were watched real close after that, especially when I was visiting my Cousins.

A Horse Called Spot

I had a horse
I called him Spot.
He couldn't run,
He couldn't trot.
Couldn't walk,
Couldn't lope.
Wouldn't hold back
On a rope.

Wobbled 'round,
Wouldn't lead.
Chewed off his ear,
Wouldn't bleed.
Branded him once,
He wouldn't kick.
Wouldn't drink water from a creek.
Wouldn't eat corn,
Wouldn't eat hay.
Rode him 60 miles a day.

Spurred his belly,
Whipped his tail,
Yanked his reins
'Till my face was pale.
Wouldn't get up,
Wouldn't whoa.
Made him a harness,
He wouldn't go.

Rode him four years
Before he was through.
Head fell off,
Tail did, too.
Broke his leg.
Cracked his back,
Carted him off
In a gunny sack.

Best damn horse
I'll ever own.
Can't find a better
Now that I'm grown.

You probably guessed
He was made of wood,
In the kitchen
Where he stood.
And I'll remember,
Like as not,
My first horse,
Whose name was Spot.

Jack Junior and Andrew Jackson Galloway

There Really is a Santa Claus

It seems if you raise little kids
There always is a problem
It happens every Christmas
So I'll bet you have to solve them.

They come home shedding great big tears
It's always just because
The other kids have told them
That there ain't no Santy Claus.

Now it happened to my little girls
So you better plainly see
This is a true story
That my mother told to me.

Sure, I came home all broken up
She said now listen here
Old Santy's always made it
Every doggone year.

If always just behave yourself
And promise to be good
Just do the very best you can
Just do the things you should.

And if you listen real close
When Christmas Eve comes round
You'll hear the sound of sleigh bells
Cause you can't forget their sound.

She looked me right straight in my eye
So I knew that she was right
Old Santy hooked up reindeer
Every Christmas night.
So don't you ever worry
She was right as you can see
"Cause Santy always gets here
And I am 63.

So Santy drives those reindeer
Just as sure as we're alive
And it's 'cause my mother told me so
And she's only 85.

One Christmas season Nancy challenged Jack to write a poem about Santa being a cowboy while she wrote one, too. Hers was published in *Western Horseman* but he didn't submit his. Jack sent her poem out in his Christmas cards that year. This is Jack's unsubmitted poem:

SANTA IS A COWBOY

Yes, Santa is a cowboy
Of that there is no doubt
But he had to figure out some things
You'll now find out about.

He was a head and heeler
He could come out with the best
But every year at Christmas time
He had to have more rest.

Cause every year these Reindeer
Gave old Santa lots of hell
And each year it sure gets tougher
To get them in the corral.

Now old Santa ain't no dummy
And he knew the reason why
It seemed his rope was getting shorter
As every year passed by.

His headin' horse had sure held up
For making all those runs
But Santa knew he's slowed down some
And something must be done.

So he sat down on his boot heels
And he chewed a bunch of Skoal
Cause he knew that this here Christmas
Would leave him in a hole.
So with whittlin' and a spittin'
The answer he had found
And this year those damned old Reindeer
Wouldn't run him in the ground.

He said it's how you call them
So on every Christmas night
They never know what day it is
And you won't have such a fight.

So every day when evening comes
He goes out to the corral
Shouts a great big Merry Christmas
And you sure can hear him yell.

And the Reindeer all come running
Cause they haven't found a way
From the way that Santa feeds them
Which one is Christmas day.

And they all hook up dead easy
Cause the Reindeer all have found
Cause every day is Merry Christmas
Whenever he's around.

The headin' horse gets lots of rest
As to Santa there's no doubt
That he sure as hell's a cowboy
Cause he figured this thing out.

So when you hear Merry Christmas
Sound big and loud this year
You'll know old Santa has them
So lookout for those deer.

Thoughts on Wrangling Dudes in Ponca State Park

A Christmas card to friends

Now here are some thoughts
That I think you should know
I came down to Ponca
'Bout ten years ago.

Now sometimes our wishes
They sure miss their mark
It happened because of
My friend Charlie Sharp.

He said come on down
The work ain't too hard
You'll never get rich
But you'll sure never starve.

So I took his word
I sure have remorses
Wound up in the park
With a bunch of damn horses.

Tied into a job
With plenty of dudes
Some of them sweet
And a lot of them rude.

Was always reminded
To have plenty of class
Beware of the state
Or be out on your ass.

So I toughed the thing out
And I'm here to say
I'm still so damn broke
That I can't get away.
So when I get to heaven
They hand me a harp
I'll blame it all
On my friend Charlie Sharp.

And if they should ask me
The truth I will tell
I'll bet you old Charlie
Is roasting in hell.

Now all of this stuff
I really don't mean
And all of this crap
Is not what it seems.

Things couldn't be better
Than they are right here
So a big Merry Christmas
And Happy New Year.

Now this note was really written
Without a bit of malice
So everyone be happy
And I'll sign this
Jack and Alice

Wranglin Dudes on Honda at Ponca State Park

How a Cowboy Knows it's Spring

Some folks have a lot of ways
To tell when spring is here,
And I've got a sure fire system,
That holds true from year to year.

Just watch a bunch of cowboys,
When the snow begins to thaw,
And the wind swings to the southward
Where it doesn't feel so raw.

These boys all get their saddles out
Start rubbin' in the grease
Sling away that busted throw rope
They don't seem to mind the least.

Send to town for some new stirrups
And a latigo or two,
Sure someone wants a brand new cinch
Calves chewed the old one through.

Each one wants new bridle reins,
Of course a good new rope.
Someone wants some saddle strings,
And a can of saddle soap.

New bridle bits, new leather gloves,
Bring a couple pairs of spur straps,
They dig up well worn Stetsons,
And throw away their fur caps.

Take to gawkin' at the horse herd
A wonderin' which and why for
Those doggone colts will break the best
And which they'd better try for.

Throw away their worn out overshoes
Tie on their spurs right neat,
They weren't in use last winter,
Cause they sure do freeze your feet.

I suppose to some poor city geek,
This wouldn't mean a thing,
But when you're seein' signs like these
Why fellers, bet it's spring.

Why I Love Nebraska

Sometimes I know you wonder
Why we love our western plains,
You say the west has vanished,
Like dust before a rain.
So sit quietly a moment,
And listen while I tell
You something of Nebraska
The range we love so well.

The morning sun is slipping
From behind an eastern hill,
It is quiet, gay, yet lovely,
Every bird and beast is still.
With a rush the spell is broken,
We hear the wrangler's yell,
That is morning in Nebraska,
Our range we love so well.

Our morning meal is over,
We walk out to the corral,
There is noise, dust and confusion,
It's the task we know so well.
See our ropes, so long and snaky,
Shooting out to catch and hold,
Some tried and gentle cow horse,
Or a fighting 4 year old.

In several months it's branding time,
The roundup's nearly done,
Hear the swish and slap of leather,
The cowboy's pleasant curse,
As he wonders to his fellows
If his cow horse could act worse.
Hear the yell of glee, from round about,
As Pete, or Bill or Ned,
Gets lost from board his fighting bronc,
Lights standing on his head.

We work all day through dirt and heat,
The dust is thick and white,
Gone our jest and fun of morning,
We are waiting for the night.
Now it's time for rest and supper,
We are tired yet happy too,
When it's sunset in Nebraska,
And our day of work is through.

The sun has passed behind the ridges,
Leaving streamers red and gold,
The hills, so black in silhouette,
Stand up so high and bold.
Then the evening star comes twinkling,
In that lovely sea of blue,
That's evening in Nebraska,
The state we love so true.

Then the yellow moon comes sliding,
Smiling down on Triple 8,
We hear the coyote's lonely wail,
The answer from its mate,
Hear the snort and tramp of horses,
Other night sounds, soft yet clear,
That is nighttime in Nebraska,
On the range we love so dear.

I'll admit it's not an Eden,
As the picture I have shown,
But just the same we love it,
Here will always be our home.
If you ever have a feeling,
You want freedom, love and friends,
Just come out to Nebraska,
Where friendship never ends.

How a Cowboy Loves The Cattle

You may think my story funny
I'm not writin' this for money
But I'm going to have my say so just the same.
You all wonder why a cowpoke
Takes his summer check and goes broke,
Playin' poker in the winter while the snowy blizzards reign.

This he does I will assure you
But most every cowboy's true blue
To the outfit that he rides the pastures for.
And you scratch your head in wonder
Then you ask us why the thunder
In the springtime he starts driftin' back to his outfit's door.

There's no mystery connected
With this boy as you expected
He just got awful tired of sittin' still,
And a sittin' there a dinkin'
He just sorta got to thinkin'
Of those little ole white faces a layin' on the hill.

Now you can start in laughin'
But he had to get back calfin'
Out those Hereford cows he always like so well.
That old chinook was siften'
So that cowboy started driftin'
Though he knew that spring was comin and he'd have to work like hell.

He loafed away the blizzard
And he didn't freeze his gizzard
A chasin' in some doggies in a storm,
He just stayed in town a restin'
And he knew it was a blessin'
To be sittin' on a counter
Where the stove was nice and warm.

He just used his head and waited
Till cold weather had abated
I'll say a cowboy's smart, you bet I will.
But when winter time was stoppin'
He just had to get a hoppin'
Where the white faced calves were poppin and a runnin' round the hill.

Becoming a Cowboy

Some think we lead an easy life,
Punching cattle day by day,
They think we work without a care,
But it never is that way.
People never seem to notice
How unsure the life we lead,
Fighting horses, stormy weather,
And the dreaded wild stampede.

Have you ever in your travels
Seen a mustang rear and fall
Over backwards on a rider,
Who has been your friend and all,
Just yesterday you cursed him
Cause he let his rope go slack,
That yearling took you in your middle.
And you landed on your back.

You were out night hawking cattle,
When the accident occurred,
Lightning dropped from heaven
Hit the middle of the herd.
The cattle start in motion
As their horns begin to pop,
There's the starting of a stampede
That's impossible to stop.

You know you're not in danger,
So you try to see in vain
What befell the other rider,
But you can't see through the rain.
Next morning just at daybreak,
You find the grim remains,
Of a pony and a rider,
Lying smashed upon the plain.

He had tried to turn the cattle,
Must have ridden in ahead,
When his horse stepped in a pup hole,
And now they both were dead.
He might have been your schoolmate,
Or your pal but still you know,
He went out in saddle,
Like he would want to go.

In the summer heat's a problem,
Horses sweat and riders swear,
If it's any hotter down in hell,
They don't want to go there.
The flies are round in dozens,
Biting horse and rider too,
You wonder if you'll finish
With the work you have to do.

In the winter, life is toughest,
We fight blizzard, ice and sleet,
When the thermometer says it's ten below,
And snow drifts three feet deep,
Calves freezing on the prairie,
Cattle starving in the hills,
Here the wolf pack wail and murmur,
As they hunt to tear and kill.

A rider's life is full of problems,
As he strives to do things right,
You bet the devil in the morning
If you're coming back at night.
Our lives are not as carefree
As songs and stories tell,
It's the only work we can do.
So we strive to do it well.

No, a rider's life is not so pretty,
He has plenty more to do
Than to ride, and look at scenery,
And rope a calf or two.
Go ahead and write your stories,
Do the very best you can,
But don't try to be a cowboy
Till you learn to be a man.

A Lesson Learned From Mick

Probably I better get this in before I forget because I believe I learned the most in the shortest time possible. Now I had been faked off, fell off, rubbed off, you name it and it had happened when I was small, but as I grew older it didn't happen much and I thought I was pretty cocky and *really* ready to try the big stuff.

We had a horse named Mick. Big, solid, bay with a lot of Hambletonian in him. I started this horse right. I know this is so because I have used that same acts and facts and rhythm ever since, and it works.

This colt was big but had been tied up, sacked out, acted nice and was ready. He bucked 3 times, plumb easy, no problem except one. I'll get to that. He was coming along as good as a colt possibly could so I turned him on the forest when I had to go to school. About a month later I came home and the horses were in the corral so I took my Mick horse out so no one could have him.

Next morning Dad sent me and one of my brothers to ride fence as some bulls had been fighting and tore it up. I would get off, drive a staple, get back on and Mick would try to buck. Next time, same thing. Now this colt was broke – no problem. I could have put him in the road, carefully eased him away and been O.K. But I thought the time had come to prove I was a big cowboy as I had already ridden him three times when he bucked.

I remember saying to my brother, "Well – here's where we see if he can buck or I can ride."

I stepped on, set my spurs as high as I could under 18 inch swells. I *think* I got started for the cantle board but I got horseback so damn fast I don't know where me, horse, or anything else went. I lost my reins, never saw his head again, and what in hell went on in between. I'm not interested, I must have still had my horn and thank goodness they were about 6 inches long because when the dust cleared away the horse had fallen in some gopher holes and then rolled me in the cactus which took me and my brother about 2 hours to pick out. That's no fun.

So here's the lesson – I learned mine good. If you get 'em broke don't go back for seconds. Or did that damn horse wait till I asked for it?

Snappin' Out Broncs on the old Flyin' U And Trying the Big Rodeo

I'm snappin' out broncs for the old Flyin' U
For 40 a month a tough buckaroo
The boss comes around and he says, say my lad
You look pretty good ridin' horses that's bad.
You see I ain't got no more outlaws to break
I'll buy you a ticket and give you a stake
At ridin' them bad ones why you ain't so slow
You might do some good at the big rodeo.

While they're a putting that bull in the chute
I'm strapping my spurs to the heels of my boots
I looked the bull over and to my surprise
I can put my whole hand between his two eyes
On top of his back there grows a big hump
I cinches my riggin' right back of that lump
I lights in his middle and lets out a scream
He came out with a beller and he starts gettin' mean.

He starts to the left but he lands to the right
But I ain't no greenhorn I'm still sittin' tight
Dust starts to foggin' right out of his skin
He's wavin' his horns right under my chin
At sunnin' his belly he couldn't be beat
He's showin' the buzzards the soles of his feet.

He's dippin' so low that my boots fill with dirt
Makin' a whip of the tail of my shirt
Snappin' the buttons right off from my clothes
A buckin' and bawlin' and blowing his nose
The crowd they're a cheerin' both me and that bull
He needed no help and I had my hands full.

He goes to fence rowin' and weavin' behind
My head starts to snappin' I sorta went blind
He starts to high divin' I let out a groan
We goes up together 'n he comes down alone
Up high I turn over and then I can see
The pawin' of dirt just waitin' for me
I picture a grave and a big slab of wood
Sayin' here lies the twister who thought he was good.

Then I noticed something don't seem to be true
The brand on his hip was a big Flying U
When I landed he charged but I still had some sense
And I get away through a hole in the fence
I'm telling you now that I'm movin' slow
I ain't goin' back to no wild west show
At straddlin' them Braymer's I swear I'm all through
I'm sure travelin' back to the old Flyin U.

My Diary

You left the river on Friday noon
That day for me was filled with gloom
For about that time it came to me
How long this week was going to be.

Things went fine till Sunday night
The kids could do the chores just right
But Monday morning all hell broke loose
What's happened since has cooked my goose.

It rained each day you sure can bet
When the chores are done you're soaking wet
Should have finished those chores real soon
But when I got through it was almost noon.

Things were going as fine as silk
When the little pigs upset the milk
I ran after them and scared the cows
Then came back and chased the sows.

I tried to cross the bridge that morn
With a bucket of milk and a bucket of corn
I slipped and fell and skinned my shin
I'll sure bet that don't happen again.

In the afternoon things quiet down
I got in the car and went to town
Looked at the mill and it was right
Got back home away before night.

Cows weren't in sight for a city block
But when I got through it was 10 o'clock.
Each time I open that granary door
Those pigs dive in including the boar.

Tuesday morning things weren't so bad
Got up at four and never got mad.
Then up to Fred's I had to race
To move his cows to the Monnier place.

Roany and I were back at six
Then I saw I was in a fix
I'll tell you this and don't you laugh
Every cow on the place had had a calf.

Four cows in the morning had seemed like heaven
But it sure was hell to come back to seven
I shut them up in that old poke corral
And got to bed a quarter to twelve.

Wednesday morning just filled with dismay
I milked the cows the whole damn day
That bob tailed cow I sure do hate her
But I finally washed the separator.

I needed a pail to make me four
And noticed one by the kitchen door
I picked it up and my whole arm hurt
For it held 12 quarts of dirt.

I dumped it out and my tummy squirms
For the thing was full of fishing worms
And can you tell me when you whistle the dogs
Why they won't come but you get the hogs?

And tell me please, right now or later,
Who left the fish in the refrigerator?
Whoever did sure shouldn't tell
"Cause when I found them they sure did smell.

To feed those calves I get real small
Like a monkey loving a basketball
They won't drink or suck or chew
I don't know what I'm going to

Tomorrow is Thursday and I can't be late
To Junior Andrews to brand at eight.
It's eleven now and I'm half dead
So I guess that I will go to bed.

In my prayers I'm going to ask
That the old black cow will have a calf
'Cause if she does I'll have three fits
From sitting out there a pulling tits.

Please hurry home from the city's charms
I'll welcome you both with open arms
You've no idea how the old time lags
Waiting here just holding bags.

Trix and the Rattlesnakes

LATE ONE AFTERNOON, OR I should say evening, Mom let me go after the milk cows. Our cows had a bell hung on their necks. As they walked they made a clatter. We could hear the bells real plain and thought they were close to the ranch buildings. The pasture is about a section and real rough, filled with hills and pretty deep canyons in one corner.

At times if the weather is very nice and quiet, sound is deceiving. This happened this evening and the cows were in the far canyon as far from the house as they could get.

I rode to the cows with no problem and started them home from the canyon. The trail there was good but only a few feet wide. The cows walked out with no problem but about half way up, Trix and I had a problem. A good sized rattlesnake was in the trail.

He was on the fight as the cows had walked over and around him and he had laid claim to the trail. It was too narrow for Trix to turn around and there was no other trail out of the gulley anyway. The snake was probably 15 feet in front of us and mad as he was, that seemed away too close.

Of course, I wanted to turn around but another rattler had staked another claim behind us and Trix and I were boxed in.

I suppose I cried a little as I knew all about rattlesnakes and was scared. Old Trix just stood absolutely still. I sat quiet. In a few minutes that seemed like an hour, the snake relaxed, quit rattling, slid off the side of the trail and disappeared. I got home with no problems so Trix taught me, don't panic. Just relax, sit quiet, and ride easy out of trouble.

The last time I remember riding Trix was to get the cows in Sand Canyon. Either the fence was down or the gate was open because the cows were out. They were strung out in the east side of the canyon so no problem except the side was real rough and rocky. I had all the cows located and was shoving them away from the rim rock and had to cross a little draw that was steep on my side.

No problem as I just told old Trix to slide down the side we were on. We slid down and he was in a lot of loose sand and rock that came down with us. He stopped and didn't move. Just stood like a statue and snorted. About then I smelled a bad odor. Have never smelled it since and don't care to. It was nothing I've run into since. Heavy and sickening. I told Trix to move and he still didn't. He very carefully worked his feet loose and by staying on the side of the hill, walked us out of there. I could have kissed him. And I had been taught another lesson – freeze up, don't panic and ease your way out of trouble.

I told this story when I got home with the cows and was told that my parents had heard there was a snake den there but didn't know where. Old Trix and I knew but we stayed out of there. In fact, that was at least 60 years ago and I never went back.

Old Horses

In those days there was no place to go with old horses. No one at our ranch could shoot them. You knew if you turned them out that they would winter kill. No one would spend money to have a horse vet put them down.

Usually we gave them to coyote trappers and they were led away. I'm sure that is what happened to old Trix although I never asked when he wasn't in the spring roundup. I just knew that a good horse had hit the big roundup in the sky.

DUKE

E WAS A WORK horse who could think. Though these words I use are mine the facts are honest and true and happened as told to me.

I never knew where Duke came from. My Uncle Charley Galloway got a hold of him somewhere to mate a mare he had, intending to make a matched team of them. They were perfectly matched but the mare was a little balky and old Duke learned to pull by pulling her and whatever he was hooked to around. They were quite large horses for that time which must have been about 1910. I imagine Duke weighed about 1,500 pounds if he was in good shape. Something happened to the mare and though no one cared about her, it left old Duke with no mate.

There was another horse there who mated old Duke for size but was dapple grey and dumb. He would pull and from then on they were always worked as a team unless Duke was being used in the breaking string as a bronc horse.

When Uncle Charley took the string of horses to Scottsbluff to dig irrigation ditches he could have taken old Duke as he and Pat belonged to him but Dad had always used them so Uncle Charley left them for him as there was just a few horses left at the old ranch and most of them were broncs or cripples.

That wasn't much for horsepower but if you had Duke and Pat hooked to something and said "Get up" something was going to move and that I *can* remember.

Now so far this is just how we happened to have this team. We had them before I can remember and I grew up with them. When I was small I didn't know you had to drive a team. I thought you just said "Get up" when you started and "Whoa" when you got there. They would listen to anyone or any voice. I know because I drove them off once when I was 3 but got caught because Dad saw me do it. I don't know if I knew how to get them stopped but I guess I knew how to start them.

Now Uncle Charley's wife was Aunt Peg. They had a little daughter, my cousin Echo. She was a baby and I was eighteen months or so old, so my Mother tells me, and able to sit between them on the seat of the buggy.

It was a nice winter afternoon and the Niobrara had been frozen over but due to some thawing days the ice had loosened and except for a small gorge here and there was clear of ice. Mom and Aunt Peg hooked Duke and Pat on the buggy and taking Echo and me drove across the river to visit Mrs. Doc Johnson on what you all know as the Sanford place.

They noticed a small ice gorge just above the ford, but it wasn't too big and they just mentioned it to each other and went on. They visited through the afternoon and started home. They noticed the gorge was quite a lot larger than it was earlier. No ice was too close so they started across. Apparently as sometimes happens, there was some sand filled ice floating beneath the surface of the water. It hit Pat nearly knocking him off his feet. He recovered just as the ice hit the buggy, turning it half around in the river and nearly over. Now the river there is quite narrow and a little deeper than the floor of a buggy. The ice hitting the horse and buggy forced it a little down stream. More ice had broken loose from the gorge and was nearly on top of them. At this ford where you come out of the river the road out is real narrow. Both up and down stream the banks are high and absolutely cannot be climbed.

The Pat horse was on the upstream side and by being hit by the ice panicked a little. The ice and heavy water had forced the team and buggy downstream away from the road with no way out of the river except upstream.

Now here is where both Aunt Peg and Mother say, "God and old Duke took over." They say he took one look at the bank they couldn't climb, shook his head, and as he was on the downstream side, simply shoved Pat around and forced him to walk upstream.

The buggy straightened out behind them, crawled slowly upstream against some ice and heavy water and walked out of the river with everything and everyone safe. They both say if he hadn't done exactly that we all would have drowned as I know myself there was no way they could have got out of there with two little kids.

Now here's the rest of the story. My Mom is 84 in Bassett and Aunt Peg is 92 in Phoenix, Ariz., and if you want to check with them I'll bet a dollar to a donut outside of a choice of words the story won't change one bit.

Duke & Pat Hauling Hay
Down The Big Hill

As you all remember, the old ranch was the place you all know as Olsen's or Van Winkle's. As you can remember there is a hill behind the house which is just a sandy cow trail and steep. At one time this was a road. They didn't use it much on leaving the buildings. They used the Cottonwood Hill east of there to go out but the one at the ranch to come down as it was so much closer.

They hauled hay down the hill with hay racks on high wheeled wagons. A little over a ton of hay doesn't seem like much now but on a hay rack is quite a load especially coming down a hill that steep. They always put on what they called a rough lock. It was a chain fastened to the rack, then wrapped around a wheel in a bunch. Then when the chain came tight it would dig in the sand and act as a brake to hold the wagon back.

One place where the hill is steepest the road was quite narrow. Cliff of rock one side straight up and about three hundred feet more or less straight down on the other. Dad was a young man at the time and had a world of confidence in old Duke and Pat. He had been hauling hay down the hill and using his rough lock. Got tired of doing it and like all of us do and having so much confidence in the team he decided to try it without the brake.

The team handled the load all right and though they were moving pretty fast at the bottom, made out O.K. Of course Dad didn't tell anyone he had pulled this stunt and continued to do the same thing on a couple of more loads with no problems. As Dad always said, "If you do something you shouldn't long enough you'll get caught." He did.

Just started down and the weight of the wagon and hay hit the horses at the steep spot. The weight broke a pole strap. That's the one strap on a harness that is there to hold a load back and without it you might just as well not have any harness at all as far as getting stopped.

The neck yoke hit Duke in the chin. The hames and collar slipped up to his ears and a ton of hay hit him from the rear. So for just a moment all the weight was on Pat and he couldn't handle any part of it. There was no where for Dad to go except along so he started talking to Duke real easy to just take it easy and "whoa" some. He saw that old horse absolutely simply plant all 4 feet, lift his rump against the front of the rack and slid all the way down the hill and stopped it at the bottom.

This is just a couple of things he did. I'll get to some more but even though we ranched for years and went through a lot of horses we never found another Duke.

Dad and the Mules

My Dad didn't like mules. He would admit very easy that mules in their own place and with someone who wanted them would be fine animals but as far as he was concerned down south in the cotton fields or the hottest spot in Hades was exactly where they belonged.

At one time or another he had mentioned mules they had owned and the trouble they had been to the ranch. In later years, with a little understanding of mule psychology, I can understand what he meant and why he was so set against them.

I had a good little rope mare named Patty Ann. One spring she got out of my jingle pasture at the Rauer place and in with Olsen's Belgian stud. Of course the inevitable, the unwanted, happened. I decided to mate her to a jack mule at the Powder Horn Ranch and made arrangements to leave her there. Mentioned this to Dad. He said to go ahead as she would probably have a good little saddle mule and they were nice to ride but if he ever caught it running loose and not tied up he would shoot it. I passed up the mule colt and as years went by I could understand why he felt that way.

As I said, the old ranch was a horse outfit and Grand Dad would buy anything and everything that was for sale in Valentine and send them out to be made into work animals. Some of this junk, of course, were mules and Dad and Uncle Charlie were to do the work.

It seems a couple of these mules were death on other animals. Dad said in a short time they killed some chickens, cats, trampled on the dogs, chewed up a little bunch of calves, and would have done the same to people if given half a chance.

I never heard what became of any of these animals, but I do know Dad and Uncle Charlie never took any of them back.

It seems Grand Dad bought a team of mules to use around the cement crew when he was building those big rock buildings on the Main Street in Valentine. This pair happened to be decent work animals. The front of those buildings have big rock in them. A lot of five hundred pound stuff and bigger in certain spots. They had rigged a boom with pulleys to get the rock up to working level and used the mules for pulling power.

They had just finished unhooking a rock when the jenny mule let out a squeal, broke loose, ran to the west end of town and dropped dead. After what happened later, I think Dad figured that was the only good mule in the world.

No one had any idea what was wrong with her, but it left the jack mule alone with nothing to mate him. As he was broke to ride, Dad was allowed to take him all over Valentine whenever he wished.

When I tell people my Dad was captured by the Sioux Indians it is true. This is what happened and probably was the start of Dad's antagonism toward mules.

Dad was born in '94 (1894) and when this happened he would have been pretty small and at that time Indians were still a little wild.

There was a big blowout of some kind taking place in Valentine and the Indians had permission to leave the reservation to attend. That meant hundreds of them coming horseback and in wagons loaded with tents and grub to stay a week or so.

Dad told me to be careful when I told it as some people wouldn't believe it, but he had seen Indian ponies with saddle sores caused by Indians' rumps as they didn't have many saddles at that time. I'm sure that was true, and it makes my rear hurt to think about it.

Valentine was small then and the Indians camped north of town and south of the creek. They would go uptown in the streets of the business area and dance. The storekeepers would come out and give them candy, etc. The next day they did it again. The mule and Dad arrived at the head of Main Street just as the Indians started to dance. Something spooked the mule and he headed down the street just as a couple of hundred Indians started to dance. Dad said the mule was cold jawed and no way could he stop him. All he could do was hang on and rattle right through the dancers, over some squaws and kids. They came out the other side still going, Dad still on, with an Indian buck hot on their tail. The mule was winded so the Indian caught him easy. Didn't do anything to Dad but led the mule into the middle of the dancers and started giving a speech. Dad said he was bawling and yelling to high heaven, didn't think there was a white man left in town as all he could see was Indians.

Finally, one of the old lawyers and a couple of other men came out and had a talk with the Indians. They led Dad and the mule out of the crowd and got them headed home. Nothing more was heard of the incident, but Dad and the mule never came out in public until after the Indians left town.

Shortly after I was born, Grand Dad sent a team of small mules to the ranch. They had been started but Dad was supposed to finish them to sell. They were coming along all right so he hooked them to a buggy and he, Mom and I started to the main ranch on the river as we still lived at the place on the hill. They had to go down the long steep slope behind the buildings. Just ahead of the hill was a gate. One of them took care of the gate and just as they stepped in the buggy one mule kicked and the runaway started. Mom jumped out as Dad told her to. She had me and Dad had the buggy and the runaway mules. They had a good head of steam when they hit the stop point of the hill.

The tongue of the buggy came out of the neck yoke and jabbed in the ground. Of course, that threw the front of the buggy into the air and even though Dad still had the lines in his hands he took off like he was shot out of a rocket as high as the lines would let him go. Mom said he was so high in the air he looked like a bird. He got hurt pretty bad, but nothing permanent. Had a bunch of broken ribs and beat up enough to gimp around all summer while complaining about anyone dumb enough to drive a team of no good mules.

One of these mules was white. She wouldn't lead and was a bunch quitter in the pasture when they jingled horses. The pasture was about half of the east side of McCann Canyon and half on the west side and real rough. Only a couple of trails to get up and down on either side. A loose horse had all the advantage of the rider and the white mule made the best of it.

One evening when Dad turned horses loose for the night he put a chain on the front leg of this mule. She raised quite a ruckus but went on to the pasture. Next morning he was using Penny to wrangle with. He could outrun anything in the country but was just getting finished as a saddle horse. He had a fault I'll get to later.

Sure enough, when the mule saw them coming she set sail across the canyon, chain and all with Dad and Penny behind. On the other side they caught up but as the mule was winded she balked and wouldn't move. Dad took the chain off and when he got her untracked they started back with the mule on the run getting hit with the chain whenever Dad and Penny caught up. This may sound rather mean, but Dad was never killer mean to anything. I've seen him awful mad but about one swat for education was all he ever took. They ran and swatted the mule clear into the corral and Dad said it must have been a good lesson. At least the mule never ran across the canyon again. Whenever she saw a rider coming she just ran home and into the corral.

This corral was on a side hill and was quite long. The mule wouldn't go in the barn so Dad roped her off from Penny intending to lead her up to harness. Again she balked, wouldn't lead and sulked. She wasn't too big so Dad decided to give her a big jerk and drag her rest of the way. Should have worked, but when the pull came Penny would rear up. Dad said he got in the habit of doing this and until then hadn't been able to get him to quit.

In the fracas Penny reared up and the mule jerked him flat. He got up, went to bucking and got jerked down again. Then when he tried to get up Dad would jump at the mule and keep him down. Dad said he did this until Penny decided to lay still and not try to get up. Took awhile but he untied them. I don't know if the mule led any better and that is the end of the mule story, but I know for sure it cured Penny of rearing. Dad said it did and I roped a lot of livestock off from him in later years and never knew him to rear or get jerked down.

Old Pal

Jack and brother Jim Galloway on Pal

OLD PAL WAS DAD'S horse. I could write a long, long time about him and never tell all of the memories the family has of him. The old ranch must have got him in "21" as he was a two-year-old then and the same age as me and I was born in "19."

A man named Cleve Thompson was working for Dad. He said a man in Kilgore had a buckskin colt that was unbroken but would probably grow into a decent work horse in time. The man also needed a look alike mate for a black horse he had. Cleve thought a sort of mean no good thing the ranch had could be traded for the colt as he would mate the trader's horse. Dad said their damn horse wasn't any good anyway so to go trade if he could.

Cleve road to town and they traded horses even up which left him afoot except for the unbroken buckskin colt. He had come off the reservation and had a big half circle on his left shoulder. We never knew where he was raised. Cleve saddled with no trouble and someone rode a ways out of town with him and he came on home alone with the big colt.

I guess Dad just liked him or something. Just started riding him because he was there. They named him Pal and he escaped the work horse string and wound up with Dad's saddle horses and eventually as his high private.

Pal had to have been an apt pupil or Dad wouldn't have kept him to ride. He was a big horse. Black mane, tail, and legs. Had a trim head, solid black hoofs. He was built big all over and gave the impression of being bigger than he really was. Probably inside of that buckskin hide was the most horse I have ever seen or will ever see.

I know it sounds trite but all horses you keep have personality and you think the world of them but on our outfit if anyone wanted to brag on a horse they had, someone would just compare him to Old Pal and the conversation usually ended. This included me.

He had a built in sense if something wasn't right. I have seen Dad ride to the river. Everyone knew Pal and would follow them in the water. If the old boy shook his head, took short hesitant steps and acted as though he would rather not go, everyone with any sense backed off and found another place to cross.

I have seen Dad tell him to go on as he needed to get across. No one ever saw Pal get down in quicksand. If he dropped in he'd just stand, the sand would settle and one at a time he would work his legs loose. Take another step, a little sip of water, work loose another step, another sip of water and work his way on out. I have seen he and Dad take the better part of an hour to cross but he would not fall. If Pal said no we believed.

We were moving cattle across the river at the Coleman place where George Drinkwalter lives. Usually behind a bunch of cattle the sand will settle, turn hard and you will be all right on any horse. The quicksand is always bad there as the river is wide and right under a high sandy bluff. A couple of horses off from the table had got down even there and they got to discussing where the sand was worst.

The people who knew the river there pointed down stream a ways and said at one time they had a standing bet of ten bucks no horse could cross there without getting down. Dad said he didn't want to bet but maybe it should be tried. Old Pal was big and stout and Dad wasn't too heavy. It was warm weather and Dad just hung his legs over the swells and they went in. Then started the pattern. Get stuck, drink a little water, work loose and repeat the process. At one time the water was up to the saddle skirts. Dad just set there, puffing his corncob pipe and they crawled up the south bank.

One guy said they should drain Old Pal because he must have drank a barrel of water as they crossed. Why he did that of course we had no idea. There are little creeks running into the river. As you rode along the bank you had to cross them and also a lot of little swamp holes. Old Pal would stop at every one and insist he have a sip of water. Wouldn't matter is they were only thirty feet apart he had to have a drink. Of course Dad would get after him because he had to keep moving but at times it was funny.

This is a little long winded but I did it so you can see why we all grew up with such absolute confidence in the old horse. Hell, if you wanted someone or something you just threw a kid or someone on him and started them out. Might take awhile but after Pal figured it out things just worked out.

At the time I'm speaking of the horses were part of the family. We of course had a Model T Ford but with just gates in fences to open, just rut roads to drive on, it was just used at special times like to get groceries at Kilgore fifteen miles away or business in Valentine, fifty or so. These were very special trips and didn't happen too often. Took a couple of weeks to get organized and ready. The rest of the time all work and transportation was built around teams like Duke and Pat, Trix, Penny, and Pal.

As I said, Pal being Dad's high private horse he was either riding or leading him constantly. Took him tied beside his work team constantly in case of a breakdown or need of some hurry up transportation.

Pal had a funny habit. As we all grew he did it a lot to all of us but especially to Dad. As you went to get on he would take a small step to the left with his left front foot. I suppose it was a reflex to take the weight of the person getting on. Anyway, just as you reached his shoulder to turn the stirrup around he would take the little step. As sure as God made little green apples he's step on one of your feet and never move.

You could beg, plead, scream, cuss or slap him, he would just stand there and wait for you to finish getting mounted. He was a big old horse and he hurt. It usually happened to Dad as he used him most. It never failed to be funny to the ones who didn't get stepped on and they usually laughed themselves sick. I have seen Pal step on Dad and Dad start to kick him in the belly with the other foot. Old Pal would turn completely around with Dad still kicking but never move that foot that was planted on Dad's toes.

Finally they would get disconnected and Dad would sit on the ground holding his foot, cussing Old Pal and telling him how someday he was going to tear off his head and hide it where he couldn't find it except he probably wouldn't miss it anyway. He never did hit the old horse after he stood up, would have shot anyone who did and there wasn't enough money in six banks to have bought him.

When Jim was small, probably about three or four, he led Pal all around while we were busy getting ready to leave. If Pal was tied up we would notice Jim was on him. We all supposed someone had set him up there. After a while we discovered no one had but he was up there. We tied Pal to the yard fence and went in the house to watch out the window. Sure enough here came Jim. Grabbed the latigo with both hands, gave a swing and hooked his bare toes just about Pal's front knee, stuck his other foot in the stirrup and crawled on up. Safe on Old Pal, he was that kind of a horse.

He and Dad taught me a lot but so much of it was when I was pretty young so it was years before I had brains enough to make use of their knowledge.

Pal was quite big and gave the impression he was clumsy. He sure wasn't but Dad helped him give that impression. They would stand and sit around at a cattle or horse roundup just resting easy. You would swear there wasn't a quick move in either one. I'm not kidding if a move was needed quick they were just a rocket exploding. After the move they would relax and sort of crawl back into position again. They fooled a lot of cowboys with this stunt and though that's where I learned it and pulled it a lot in later years myself, I never made it work like they could. Of course, I never had another Pal.

He was a cow sorting fool. When he was working a herd at his best he looked and acted half asleep. Of course Dad wanted him that way. They worked slow and quite a ways off their cattle but nothing came back by that old horse. I have seen a few fighting cattle hit him in the chest and get by but it was damn well after they hit him cause he was a big bump to run over and was usually there.

In later years Dad never used a bridle on him. I'm sure of this because I ran off with the only bridle bit I ever knew Dad to have and he never took it away from me. Still have it.

One time I found an old bridle bit. Took some junk strings from the house and made me another bridle. When Dad asked me how come I said maybe my horse would like the bit better. Then he gave me one of those quick answers I talk about. He said, "Hell, kid, the bit in a horse's mouth don't mean a thing. You could put a corn cob in Old Pal's mouth and get just as much work done." I never found that wrong. Through the years I'm sure I broke a few pretty good horses but was forty years old before I made enough money to own more than two bridle bits.

It used to seem like I spent all my time on a saddle horse trailing Dad in the lunch wagon, team in front and Pal tied with a halter on the side of the team. Seemed like there was always a little fence to fix, posts to haul, something to be hauled even though we were going to ride pastures.

We might even be going to sort cattle to ship but the team still went along. We'd get to the cattle, leave the team, Dad take Pal with just his halter and go to work. I really think he would have worked as well with a rope around his neck.

Though Pal could move, he intended to use his energy to his best advantage. He could turn on a dime if necessary but that was when he decided it was necessary. You could be loping down the road and decide to turn around and go back. Of course you could but that was after you yelled whoa four times, jerked the reins four times, waited six seconds for Pal to decide you really meant it. Then he would stop and start to turn so slow you felt like getting off and turning him by hand. He could run and he could move if necessary but he never wasted a single move.

In later years he was the damndest thing to rope off from you ever saw. In sorting he stayed off his cattle and when you were roping he did the same thing. He absolutely would not run up except so close to a critter. We all carried thirty-five feet ropes and intended to use it all but not on Pal. A forty-five footer would have been about right as he was taking no chance on that critter coming back by him. He was trained to keep them in front of him and the farther the better. Eventually the animal would get winded and you could get it roped and tied to Pal. He could outrun cattle alright but didn't take the chance of them coming back by him.

If you were riding along a fence and decided you wanted to get on the other side it was no problem for Dad and Old Pal. Sometimes it would be two or three miles to a gate. If the fence was really tight Dad might have to kick out a staple in the top wire. Sometimes they were still looking a little high but he would tell Old Pal to crawl over. Pal knew he had plenty of time and always took advantage of the fact. I swear he would take a good five minutes to get to the other side. He never had a scratch on him.

One time we pitched hay over the fence at the barn. It was winter so not much stock was at the place. Seemed like we were always short on hay so turned everything we could out in the hills till spring. We fed the few cattle there and could see Pal up on the hills by the fence just standing there. An hour or so later as he hadn't moved we went up to see why. Some way he had put his foot over the bottom wire but never moved after he did it. We didn't have any idea when he got trapped. Sometime during the night Dad just picked his foot out and he loped down to feed. Most horses would have been cut.

When Andersons left the river to move to Kilgore, Dad, Jim Hendershot and I drove the cattle to town. It was in the fall and a heavy cloudy day. A light mist was falling and we were afraid it might snow a little. We all had chaps and heavy coats but even then you were pretty uncomfortable when not moving.

For some reason we had to hold the herd for about an hour waiting for the milk cows. We were getting cold and stiff just standing or sitting so decided to do something to get warm. Didn't want to run foot races with so many clothes on but Jim and I decided to rope a yearling steer and ride him. They let me have the rope as we only had one and I was lucky and caught the steer. Jim took a set at him. He and I were warm so Dad took the rope to catch one for me to ride as he was still cold.

Dad didn't rope much off from Pal. He was a good pasture roper but as I was usually along he let me rope whenever he could.

They cut out a steer and he started to run down a cow trail. That was the one time I guess either Pal went to sleep or didn't realize Dad intended to catch the critter, He loped to the steer, the steer turned out perfectly to the right, Dad roped him. Pal wasn't watching Dad, Dad wasn't watching Pal and expected him to turn behind the steer. None of this took place.

Pal just kept loping down the trail with Dad still watching the steer and when the slack came out of that rope you could hear it pop for half a mile. The steer hit the rope broadside to Pal jerking him sideways out of the trail. Dad went straight up, turned a complete somersault in the air and came down flat on his back in front of the whole fracus.

Jim and I rode over as fast as we could expecting to find Dad hurt some but though he got up pretty slow, he wasn't hurt at all. Shook up some but the heavy clothes had padded the fall. As he wasn't hurt, we thought it was hilarious. Told him to either ride slower or hang on tighter. Pal was still standing there holding the steer. Dad walked up to him and said, "You old S of a B, maybe next time you'll wake up."

I rode the steer, we were all warm, took the cattle on to Kilgore but that was one time Old Pal slept too long.

72

The winter of '33 or '34 we didn't have hardly any hay. No rain during the summer and grass was short. We only had about forty cows to take care of, a couple of winter milk cows, two saddle horses and a work team. I could mow ten acres a day and Dad could haul it away in one load and not a very big load either.

The sand in the real Sandhills has a way of sort of holding moisture so out on the Forest Reserve the grass was good as it was over grazed. The first division south was a pretty big pasture. Probably between nine and eleven sections with no cross fences. They gave Dad a winter permit in there for forty head of cows. He banked the middle well so it wouldn't freeze, took out a triple box wagon of cattle cake and turned his cows in about December first.

Some of us would ride the three or four miles out every day all winter, open the tank and give them a pound of cake. It was a devil of a job when the river was frozen but we managed.

The cows started to calve but had to stay there as there was no feed any place else. If a cow was missing there wasn't much you could do unless there was some snow on so you could track her. Eventually she would show up with her calf. It doesn't seem possible but in the spring all forty cows were still alive, every one had a calf on her, and they were really in pretty good shape. Fortunately these were all young cows and we had an open winter.

Now back to Pal. I was going to high school and was home for the weekend. It was real cold in the dead of winter and I went to cake the cows. Dad always used Pal and if his feet were cold, he would step off, get behind Pal and grab his tail. They would walk down a trail till Dad was warm. Very few horses will do this and not run off. I had seen them do this a lot when I was along but they did it when they were alone.

I had fed the cattle and started home. Facing that northwest wind, my feet were cold and though I was real allergic to walking I decided to do it as Dad had reminded me I could before I left.

I get off, grabbed his tail and he stood still. I told him to go on and he just stood looking over his shoulder at me. I poked him in the rump and I guess that was the wrong thing to do. He lit out for home on a high lope leaving me afoot a couple of miles out in the big Sandhills. He would have stayed there all day if I hadn't poked him.

Fortunately for me, there was one fence between us and the river. When I caught up, my feet were warm and so was my temper but I just opened the gate for him and rode on home. If I walked with Pal after that, I walked and *he* followed. Dad still did it but it didn't work for me.

All of our saddle horses, after they were broke, would stay around close wherever you dropped their reins. We never made a point to try and teach them to do this but most all family horses will just graze around during the day and still be close by in the evening when you went to go home.

All except Pal. If you dropped his reins he would always walk off about a hundred yards before he started to graze. Go get him, move ahead, drop the reins, same thing again. No trouble to catch, never left, but always with that distance to graze if you turned him loose ten times a day. We used to think Dad always took a kid with him just to go get Old Pal after he walked off.

I'll probably mention him later but he lived to be an old horse. He had retired and not used for a few years but we always kept him near plenty of feed and water. I had him at the Rauer place at about forty ton of hay in the stacks. The creek never froze and he could always get water. I had grain in my hand and called him. He came to me and when I turned my back I heard a funny sound. Jumped sideways as Old Pal wilted and lay down.

It must have been a heart attack if horses have them because he never moved a muscle. I felt real bad but was sort of glad I was there as I knew he went with a full belly and didn't suffer.

Old Pal and The Hogs

For some reason Old Pal hated hogs. He would have been unhandy in a state like Iowa. We didn't raise many but what we had were usually loose around the place. The corral and barn were Pal's stomping ground and if any hogs tried to get in his territory he really put the run on them.

He found some in the barn and put the run on those, too. I was just coming in the door. First the hogs ironed me out and Pal was right behind them with his mouth wide open. I managed to roll out of his way so escaped but he sure hated them. Of course, we never knew why.

He liked fresh milk. In the summer time we milked out in the corral. If Pal happened to get or be loose, a fresh bucket of milk was just gone. He could drink sixteen quarts in about three swallows and barely burp.

One time Dad was shipping hogs out of Kilgore. In the summer they always moved hogs at night as they would get too hot during the day. They had special wagons for this job and the twelve or fifteen miles to Kilgore took quite awhile as the horses were pulling a lot of weight. Dad had milked before he left about midnight.

Next morning Mom had to milk alone, and though I remember this very plain, I wasn't big enough to help. This was at the old ranch. Mom had filled two sixteen quart buckets with fresh milk and they were hanging on the barn wall. It was real hot and the milking had taken Mom quite awhile and I thought she was never going to finish.

She had just finished the last cow and had another bucket full. That corral was large and we were quite a ways from the hanging buckets. Old Pal was loose there and discovered the milk just as she finished. We yelled and hurried toward him but he never moved, just shut his eyes and drank. Slurped up the thirty quarts or so of milk before we could chase him away.

It was disappointing to Mom to lose the milk after that much work but the separating didn't take long and Old Pal was probably the happiest horse on the Niobrara River.

He had a thing about someone getting on him from a corral fence or a bank or anything else except the ground. He would stand absolutely still to be mounted from the ground. You could crawl up his rump or anything else as long as you started from the ground. As good as he was he wouldn't let you ride up to a fence and put someone on behind you. I saw he and Dad have a lot of fights about this but Pal always won.

Dad and I started across the river after a load of wood. He was driving Ben and Jerry. Kind of a good looking team that traveled real well but once in awhile would balk. At least Ben would and then Jerry would refuse to pull also. Ben had been broke to ride but wouldn't quit bucking so they broke him to work. Along the way he had learned to balk.

He and Jerry were so perfectly matched they were always worked together. The fact that they would balk at times was the reason Uncle Charley hadn't taken them to Scottsbluff to use on the irrigation ditches.

We started across the river and the water was about axle high on the high wheeled wagon. It was empty except for Dad and his axe but Ben froze up and quit. Probably hit a little quicksand or something. Jerry refused to pull so there they were. Dad didn't do anything to them as he had been the route before. Just cussed a lot as he knew he would have wrangled another team to go after the wood.

We never tied our neck yokes to the wagon tongue so Dad just pulled the pin on the eveners, the wagon tongue fell down, the team turned around and went to the bank and Dad was dry but still in the wagon.

It was early winter just cold enough to have a little ice on the bank and a little slush in the river. Of course, Dad didn't want to strip and wade out in that cold water and as I, as usual, was trailing along on Pal. Dad told me to ride up and pick him up. I know Dad figured that out in the cold water Pal would forget about not wanting mounted from a fence.

I rode up close to the wagon and Dad started to get on behind me. He was quite short legged anyway and just as he was stretched out and had reached the point of no return, Pal moved. Not much but enough to cause Dad to lose his balance. His feet were up, his head was down and he went plumb out of sight in the cold water. He was all right but came up soaking wet and yelling to high heaven about damn dumb kids and damn dumb horses

He didn't do anything to either Pal or I. Just headed for a fire and dry clothes. I came on in with the work team. I don't remember how the wagon got home. I do know Ben and Jerry were never hooked again on our place and Dad sent them to eastern Nebraska with a horse buyer who came by the next spring. Also none of us ever tried to get from a wagon to Old Pal's back in the river, in winter time.

Pal could run. As I mentioned he and Dad always gave the impression of being half asleep. It was just an act they had down pat as a lot of animals and people would agree. Dad was about as strict as to how we handled the horses and cattle as a man could get. I mean, you worked slow and quiet with no unnecessary fuss, but when you were going home afterwards you were allowed one short horse race or most any fun thing you could think of.

Before the other kids were big enough to go along it was usually just Dad and I alone. I always wanted a horse race always hoping to some time outrun Pal. Dad would pick out a post or some marker not far away to run to. I got beat but once or twice we almost had a tie, I thought. Finally he agreed to a head start for me. He'd yell go and of course Old Pal was moving and past before my horse woke up. Then I got to yell go but would forget to wake up my horse before I yelled.

Once I yelled go and got a good start. Looked back and Dad and Pal we were just loping along. He yelled "Wait for me," I did and they went by me like a freight train past a bum. He taught me good because by the time I was old enough to ride races I knew most every trick in the book.

At the fall "Happy Day Picnic" they had what they called a free-for-all "Brush and Swamp" race. It was designed to separate the speed horses from just good saddle horses and give more people a chance for some money.

It started on the regular hard land quarter mile race track, then dropped over a rather steep fifty feet bank into a swamp about belly deep on a horse and pretty sticky but safe enough if handled slow. The swamp was about a hundred and fifty feet wide. Then they were to turn east for a quarter of a mile through almost a jungle of trees, high weeds and under brush. They had tied a lot of small flags on the brush and trees so the racers could tell where to go. Then they were to turn south, back across the swamp, back to the starting point and again up the quarter mile of hard track to the finish line.

It was a race to really try out a horse for sure to run in it but Dad took me and my horse out of the way and told me to damn well stay there as he was in the race himself. That was news to me but actually the committee had sent Dad along as a sort of judge to report if a racer didn't follow the race pattern or did something illegal. No one else knew that was the reason he was there. We found that out afterwards.

Happy Days Picnic Poster

They started and ran the first quarter and when they turned toward the river and swamp were in a fair bunch. A couple of fast horses out in front. A few slow ones in back, quite a bunch in the middle which is where Dad was. He and Pal giving the impression of just loping along on the way to church. After they made the turn they were out of sight until they came back to high ground where the race had started.

I didn't stay where I was told to and rode toward where I knew the race was to come back in sight. First horse in sight was Pal, Dad on top still loping along like they were coming home from church.

Honestly, it was a good ten seconds before another horse showed up. Dad just came to the side of the track and stayed as he was a judge and not a contestant. Pal had quite a lot of mud on him but wasn't even blowing hard. They could have won that race by a hundred yards. I was mad at Dad and yelled because he didn't finish the race. He said it wouldn't have been fair as he was a committee member and just rode along to be a judge. Besides, he and Pal had been over the ground when they were both young. I suppose that meant ten years before.

I know because I looked in later years. I know that Dad and Pal went exactly where that race was supposed to go because there was no other way out.

Dad was small, a good rider, and sure as hell must have been mounted on a sure enough horse because they flat out ran the rest of that bunch and never took a deep breath.

ANOTHER PAL STORY

PAL COULD PULL AND would pull on a rope. He was solid as a big old tree if you roped a critter and would pull them most anywhere you wanted to go but he hated to pull dead weight.

Once in awhile we would want to move an empty wagon or hay rack and not want to harness a team. They moved easy so we would just use a saddle horse. No problem except when the horse was Pal. We would get the rope on the tongue, dally the horn and tell Pal to go. He would tighten the rope till the wagon tongue was off the ground, then bunch his muscles, plant his feet, put his head down and groan like he was being murdered. You could hit the rope and it would be plumb slack. That was if I was on him when I was small.

Then Dad would take over and the same thing would happen. Then Dad would tie hard and fast leaving the end of the rope loose to show Pal he intended to warm his rump. After he explained to Pal exactly what he was going to do if that wagon didn't move and away they would go.

I honestly don't think Pal ever did get hit but he and Dad understood each other. I'll bet I saw this happen twenty five times on different pieces of machinery and every time it was a repeat of the past.

Horses Should Not Be Afraid

WHILE THE SUBJECT OF horses not being afraid is so important I will mention an odd thing that happened to Lucky and I.

Lucky was a little, real solid, sorrel horse with a wide strip in his face and a couple of white hind feet. Weighed about a thousand pounds in riding shape. He was out of the little Anderson mare who was also the mother of Patty. Dad traded Andersons out of him when they came down from Whitney to get their horses that we had been keeping through the years. Lucky just had one fault I ever found. I never could figure why, but you absolutely could not trim his tail. You could curry it, shake it, pull a couple tail hairs and he would throw a fit. Quite often his rear end looked like a haystack looking for a place to settle. Finally I would tie up a hind leg and trim his tail. Even then it was a hassle and you had to watch his other feet real close.

He was probably the first horse I ever did put a good breaking job on. Broke him at two years old and just used him on short rides like getting milk cows and jingling horses. He was a real apt pupil. I just saddled him and rode off. He never did buck. He wasn't too fast in a race but was solid, always in condition, as we used him with grain all the time. You could sure get what you went after. He sorted cattle plumb good and was very solid on a rope. I used him a lot snaking corral poles out of those big canyons.

Nancy and Lucky were the same age. We lived on the Rauer place and our dogs, cats, and ranch animals were her neighbors and friends who came to visit. Lucky was always so gentle, she was either on top of him or leading him around. Of course, they kind of grew up together and he was considered her horse unless we had to have him for some reason. That sometimes led to a lot of explaining and didn't always work.

One day we were eating dinner and I broke the news that I had to have Lucky that afternoon. Nancy left the table a little early and when we

81

finished our meal discovered that she and the horse were both missing. We weren't worried as she and Lucky rode all around the place and out in the pasture. I saddled old Doc, a work horse I had broke to ride when I was a kid, and rode out to find her and also to get Lucky as I had to have him. Sure enough, they were in a pocket in some trees. The wind was blowing a gale and she didn't hear me coming. Then asked her what she was doing. She said she was hiding from me. I told her I guessed she was caught and had to be "it" in the next game and we went home. This isn't important except that Lucky was so good with her that we weren't worried at all while I was finding them.

As I remember, Lucky only fell over once with me in all the time I used him. I had him in and out of some rough places, but he was real solid on his feet. No one, as far as I know, has been able to figure out why the best footed horse in the world will be walking along, tangle up and fall flat. Some horses stumbled a lot but hardly ever fall, but a real good horse, for some reason, will tangle up on level ground and really fall hard. I've sure seen it happen a number of times. Maybe they go to sleep. One guy said they just get tired.

Anyway, Lucky and I had been caking cattle on the Forest Reserve and were on our way home. It was pretty cold and I was dressed for it and was real comfortable. It was snowing real hard, but no wind. I had on chaps, sheepskin coat, and heavy mittens. I had my Hamley saddle and they made their stirrups a shade smaller than most so you wouldn't be apt to get a foot through them. I had mine leather covered which made them still tighter. Also, I had on overshoes. I would ride on the balls of my feet and knew the overshoes could be forced into the stirrups but was comfortable not to do so because I knew I could get hung up.

Nancy on Lucky

We were walking down a wagon road. About three inches of fluffy snow on the ground and coming down heavy. Lucky tangled up for some reason and fell. I mean quick and in a heap. Just like he'd been shot. I went off the right side. As we hit the ground I felt my overshoes go through the stirrup and knew I was hung up. Of course I was reaching for the reins as I hit the ground but with the heavy mittens couldn't have done anything with them anyway. I did capture one, but was on the ground on my back in the snow. My right foot caught in the stirrup. Lucky took about a step and I told him "Whoa." He stood still and I rolled against his front leg, got enough pressure against him to stand up on my leg and work my overshoe out of the stirrup.

I suppose if he had spooked I would have come loose somewhere but I would have probably not been in very good shape and still four miles from home afoot. Lucky for me I had followed Dad's advice because Lucky wasn't scared.

While I have been on the thoughts of horses not being scared I want to bring up a little mare I had in later years named Bitsy.

She was out of Wayne Cornish's old bay roping mare that made him so much money and was named Top Rodeo Horse of the Year in South

Dakota. Some of that was a credit to Wayne's talent, but they also used her to dog and line steers. She had a vicious temper and would buck most any time even on a rope, but was so good she still took them to the pay window real steady. It had taken Wayne and Skinner Robertson all summer to break her and they changed off. I once saw Wayne rope a calf in Merriman. He threw his slack, stepped down and got to the calf. The old mare let out a squeal like a wounded panther, hung her head and bucked up the rope to the calf and stopped. No reason at all, she was just that way.

She was out of the Hay Valley horses. They brought in probably the first registered Quarter Horse stud in Cherry County. They just got too many horses and sent a few truckloads of young ones to the plant at North Platte. That's where Harry Cornish found her, bought her, and gave her to Wayne.

That was Bitsy's mother and her dad was a registered stud he dogged off from. After I traded for the colt I always said I was going out to feed my little bitty horse. Alice named her Bitsy and though she inherited a few of her mother's temperamental traits, turned into a real good horse or at least we thought so.

Bitsy was born late in July. That's a little late in the year, but as I knew it, all of her training was about a year later than on most horses. Consequently she was about a year older than average as I brought her along.

Of course I had intended to make a rope horse out of her, but as I came to Ponca to wrangle horses at the state park she just turned into a saddle horse. She was four years old at the time.

I was working for the sale barn in Valentine and had bought a mare from Ray Bennett just to use there because I didn't want to use Snip or Princess as we were rodeoing pretty steady with them.

Wayne was getting too many young horses and Bitsy couldn't be registered. Decided to get rid of her. Actually, she was a full blood Quarter Horse but the papers hadn't been kept up on her ancestors. Wayne's wife Phyllis had made a pet out of Bitsy all of her life which was about eighteen months when I traded for her. Phyllis had never tied her up or led her but she was real gentle and would follow wherever you walked. Wayne was going to send her through a sort of a junk sale at the sale barn. Phyllis threw a fit and wouldn't let him. She insisted they find a home for her or they had to give her away. I had told Wayne I might buy her if she didn't go too high. He came around and told me as he had to get along with his wife would I trade the mare I was riding for the colt. I had never seen her but I only had eighty-five bucks in the mare. We traded and he brought her in the next morning.

Jack on Bitsy

I never did really make an attempt to break her at all. She was always in the road when we grained horses. We just petted and loved her to death. Of course, I was a lot older by this time and more interested in pets than bringing on a finished horse. I did lead her some and tied her a few times, but as she resented being tied, I just didn't do it.

She had been saddled three or four times and would usually pull loose from me and buck around the corral a couple of times. I thought it was kind of cute and would pull up the cinch, ride a few minutes and turn her loose. I suppose that's why she was a little ornery later but she was never scared. Just had her own way of letting you know she was unhappy.

I had been at the Ponca Park for a couple of weeks getting horses ready for trail rides and they asked me to give a talk on horses to a 4-H club. I don't suppose my talk was too much, just demonstrated tail trimming and hoof care as I had been taught by the old boys. I used Bitsy for an example and make out okay on the tail trimming as she really needed it. When I started on the feet I guess she figured she had done her part and refused to let me have them. I just changed horses and went on, but when I finished I decided it was time she and I came to an understanding about a few things as she was old enough to break.

I tied her up with some gear she wouldn't break and the battle was on. Eventually she had a foot tied up, a saddle on, and was about as mad as a little horse could get. I turned her loose from the post and she bucked and bawled all over the place and finally fell down on the side where the leg was tied. I just sat on top of her while we both got our wind. Finally got the tie loose, she got up and I led her to the corral. She would always pull back and break anything on her head if she could, but if she couldn't she would never try twice. Never had any more trouble about the feet and the next morning saddled up and she rode away. She never bucked the rest of the summer and in the fall when we shut off the rides she was real well broke.

You could catch her with anything that rattled. I used to catch her with those little tiny Tic-Tacs in a plastic box. She was always in the corral at the park and kids from the city would run to the fence to see her. She thought everyone was her friend and they taught her to eat anything. She loved candy, cookies and any fruit. She never bit anyone except David's bare toe. She would drink pop out of a can if you held it up for her. She was real handy to use fixing fence in the breaks. You just dropped the reins and she would just graze around. I have left her for a couple of hours and she was still there when I came back.

The next spring I came down to get ready to take out rides and brought Bitsy with me. Sometime during the fall and winter they had put down a new well. To get a level place for the well they had dozed a spot and shoveled the loose dirt over the bank. It had been raining a lot and the dirt turned to goopy mud. To a person from the Sandhills this mud is something else.

I couldn't believe you could get a car stuck with a back wheel only an inch off from an oil mat, but you sure can. I swear, I slid down the hill into half the trees in the park and my pickup had fenders to prove it. Eventually, I learned but it was a hard lesson. This was 15 years later and I cannot believe the stuff.

Bitsy and I started around and across the spot where they had pushed the fresh dirt. The weeds had grown up thick and about a foot high. With no warning she was in up to her belly and very surprised. I figured we would work our way out so I sat still. She lunged a couple of times, her feet stuck and she fell. I had made no attempt to get off and was still in the saddle. Her back was downhill in the mud. No way could she get up except by rolling over me and getting her feet downhill.

I'm still in the saddle with my left leg under her and she was laying on my leg. The mud was soft enough I wasn't hurt, but I could not get loose. If she had fought or struggled she would have rolled over me, which she could have done as her feet came loose when she fell and were pointed up hill. She never moved a muscle except her head.

I knew there were some men working there close so started yelling for help. They could hear me but the terrain distorted the sound enough they couldn't find where we were. Except for yelling I didn't try to move and Bitsy would pick up her head and look over her shoulder at me. I would push her head down flat and say, "You're O.K. little horse, but I'm in a hell of a shape."

She probably did this three times, but never struggled. My cinch ring and short latigo were on top of her, but just out of my reach. Very, very carefully I wiggled loose enough to reach the latigo, afraid if I wiggled she would move too but she never did. I managed to unbuckle the latigo. I was sure glad I had the habit of not pulling my cinches too tight. It is not a good habit to have, but got me out of the mess as I could get enough slack to work the buckle. When the saddle came and we both were loose, Bitsy was able to get up easy and we walked out. Saddle, me, and Bitsy. Covered with mud, but safe. Bitsy wasn't scared.

MICK AND THE RIVER

DURING THE DROUGHT IN the '30s we were usually short on hay and would leave the cattle on the Forest Reserve as long as possible. Until the snow got too deep to graze we would just ride out every day and give them a pound or so cottonseed cake. They watered at the river creeks as water was no problem.

I was in high school and home for the weekend so I took the horse, Mick, and went to cake these cows. It was a long two miles west to the ford which I used to go over. The cows were just across the river from the ranch, which made me only a quarter of a mile from home but the river was in-between.

I fed the cows and it looked like a long way west to the good ford. I was on a high hill and looking down at the river could see where the channel of open water hit the south bank where I was, and then stayed open to the north bank and there was no ice there.

We sometimes crossed the river at this point in the summer and though it was a little deep had never had any trouble. The channel was probably about thirty feet wide and on the down stream side completely covered with ice.

There was about a three foot straight down bank on the south side where I had to get in the river, but no ice and the north bank was not steep.

I rode Mick to the south bank, told him to jump in. He never hesitated, just jumped. He went completely out of sight in the water and my first thought was he had hit quick sand and fallen. As he bounced to the surface I stepped off on the upstream side but did happen to keep a good hold on the horn of the saddle. Of course I was up to my armpits in water with sure no sand or anything solid under my feet. I was just hanging there and that ice on the downhill side was getting closer.

Of course what had happened was the river had just cut a channel in the ice and the whole damn thing was running in that narrow span. That's a lot of water in a narrow space.

Mick just shook his head and with me hanging on his side, swam to the north bank and crawled out. Lucky for us both he was a big stout young horse. That ice on the downstream side was only a few feet away when we hit that bank.

If that horse had panicked or hesitated one moment I wouldn't be writing this.

He wasn't scared.

Biting Mares

WE HAD A TEAM of mares. Just a good team of horses. Pete Galloway broke the grey we called Roxy and George Monnier broke the bay we called Lady. As young mares they were all right but as they got older they started to bite.

It was honestly funny to watch someone else try to put up a neck yoke. We had a couple of hired men who wouldn't work them at all.

When you tried to pick up the tongue they would both bite at you. They were smooth and fast as striking snakes. If a person held the head of one, the other would bite you. Then both of you would get on the outside of one horse and get the neck yoke fastened. As you went to the other outside, both mares would snap at you. Finally with both men on the outside of the second mare and got the neck yoke fastened. After that they were all right until the neck yoke was dropped and you started over. These mares were all-day horses and wouldn't hurt a fly except at hook up time.

One time I saw Dad decide to put a stop to it. He had a hardwood stick about the size of a pitchfork handle and two feet or so long. An old mare would bite and get bopped, then the other and get bopped, then he'd hold out the stick and they'd bite it. I thought it was about as funny as anything could get. They were getting hit hard enough to hurt but never slowed down or gave up. After a half an hour or so, the stick was about chewed up and Dad got tired of bopping and the old mares won the battle of the wagon tongue.

We had them around for a few more years but quit using them as a steady team when some younger stuff came along with a better disposition. We never had any horses do this before or afterwards. No one can ever guess why just those two or why they were that way.

I think the bay was turned to the Forest in the fall and winter killed. The grey was a little younger and we traded her and a one-eyed black horse named Nig on our first Model A Ford. I'm sure of that because I rode Nig and led the mare to Kilgore after the deal was made.

TOM AND JERRY

THIS IS JUST ANOTHER chain of facts that happened that I have never been able to understand.

One of the colts was from Patty and the other from Butterfly. Their dad was a Thoroughbred stud that Loyd Olson had. Shorty Weber had him to use on the Rothleutner mares and let me turn mine in with them for a couple of months.

I started these colts at the same time the summer they were two year olds. They both started real easy. The Tom colt out of Butterfly always had a little buck in him but was just cold backed at saddling. He couldn't buck off a wet saddle blanket, but he was always a little limber legged and I only used him on short easy rides.

The Jerry colt from Patty was quite small but a real stout little horse. Never bucked at all, just went to work like an old horse but was real awake under a saddle. I thought a lot of him and used him the winter when he was coming four.

I had him sharp shod all the way around as there was a lot of ice that winter. Some times that damn river would freeze out a good ways from both banks and stay open the middle. With a shod horse you could ride out on ice, jump in the river water, jump up on the ice on the other side and go on.

The day was clear but awful cold and I had on all the winter clothes I could carry. We jumped in the open water all right but then hit a little quicksand and the current was quite strong. Jerry went down on his side with his back down stream. I stepped off on that side and let go of my reins to stay clear of him.

We all have seen horses buck a cowboy off at a rodeo or other place and then chase him. It isn't meanness always, just fear or a nervous reaction to strange surroundings or what is happening. Dad said he thought it was from fear and they wanted to get close to something they felt safe with. Whatever it is, it happened to Jerry.

Jerry had never ever done a mean thing but the river water rolled him completely over and he came up scared to death. Luckily I was far enough away to stay clear but he started to lunge and strike coming at me. I tell you he looked ten feet tall and those sharp shoes looked big as wash tubs. The water was a little better than waist deep and I managed to roll up on the ice. I rolled a ways and stood up. Jerry jumped up also, quit striking and came to me. We headed home to the barn and dry clothes but I still don't really know why horses pull this stunt, but they sure do.

I also have never known why other people's horses never buck with me and mine usually bucked with other people. It was always that way. I suppose it was a fault in my breaking but as they didn't buck with me or my family, I've never known what it was.

When I left the ranch in '48, I sold both these horses to Floyd Jones. Got forty bucks a head for them. Hated to let them go but I was leaving and couldn't take them with me. Also the price was pretty good.

Jones sold the Tom horse to a big outfit. He bucked a couple of guys off and got to bucking so hard they gave him back. Jones rode him some with no trouble and he was struck by lightning. Jones said there was no justice as there was twenty head of horses in the bunch and the lightning got the only one he owned.

He sold the Jerry horse to a pretty good cowboy and repeated what I had told him. Don't cinch him too tight in the morning because he don't buck. Tighten it later. The cowboy decided he could cinch any way and time he pleased and proceeded to do so. Sure enough, he came apart just as I said he would and in a month they had him in Peterson's bucking string.

Why the horses turned out that way you can kind of understand but they hadn't caused me any trouble and with a little T.L.C. I don't feel would have caused them any either.

TIM

WHEN PETE GALLOWAY SOLD out on the old Chafin place, John Joseph sold a black saddle horse on his sale. Dad bought him for Jim to ride to school. He was gentle and a nice horse to have around but resented being mounted double, which was a must on our outfit. He also was a little rough riding so no one fell much in love with him and he was turned out on the forest with the wild bunch.

We had plenty of horses coming on and hadn't had any colts for a couple of years. There was something about the horse we didn't know and hadn't been told. Don't know if Joseph knew it or not but the next spring the wild mares all came in very pregnant. This horse had never shone any interest in mares when we were riding him but must have been able to become a daddy. They were probably the nicest looking colts we had ever had but didn't need them so got rid of their daddy.

When the colts were two years old there was one I really liked. He was built real solid but had trim legs and head. Not one white hair on him. I named him Tim and kinda kept him for myself. There was four of these colts that I started the summer they were two. Didn't try to teach them anything, just rode them to the hayfield and jingled horses on them in the mornings. I broke them to hobble so they could eat during the day then keep them in to wrangle the next morning, then change colts.

I had started three of them but left Tim till last. His mother was a mean old thing and her colts always had a mean streak of some kind. We had broke a couple of them to work and they were nothing but trouble. I expected him to be the same way and though he had broke to lead real nice I expected the mean streak to show up when I saddled him.

I never did like bronc rides but was short on time so after I got my nerve up decided to saddle him, stick both spurs in his shoulders and if I was still

94

on top when the dust cleared I would go on with him but if I was bucked down would just turn him loose.

Led him out north of the house in the open. One of the kids was along to haze for me. Stepped up on him, set myself as best I knew how, stuck both spurs in his shoulders and expected the worst. I have never been more surprised or ashamed of anything as I was at the next few moments. He just sort of loped away because he didn't know what else to do. Head was up, he was kind of looking back at me with a hurt look in his eyes that said, "Why did you do that to me, and what did I do?" He never bucked a jump in his life and I was so ashamed of me he probably got more petting and easy handling than any colt I ever started.

I was raised on a rule of thumb as to how to ride young horses. You were to start them at two years old and do nothing with their heads. Just easy, short rides. Turn them out to graze in the winter. The spring at three years old you were to start to train them during the summer. You rode them and grained them all winter until the spring they were four. When the grass was green you turned them out on pasture until late in the fall. Then bring them in for a winter horse. I had never had a chance to try this until the year Tim came along but by that time we had plenty of horses so I was able to try it this way.

I usually don't know if it will work out but it sure worked fine on him. He turned out real, real gentle. Grew into a good sized saddle horse, perfect saddle horse, and a little bit gaited. In the fall Alice and I won the rescue race on him at our little rodeo the summer he was four. That's the time I tore the seat out of her jeans getting her mounted.

I know horses can't really figure out to do odd things but I knew Tim to do a couple of odd stunts. As I said I kept a horse in the corral at night to use the next morning. They were just loose in there with the milk cows. One night I was milking late and it was dark. One of those nights when you can't even see the ground. I would just walk around until I bumped into a cow and milk her. Tim was in that night and black as he was, he was invisible.

I was completely relaxed, half asleep, with the milk pail between my legs. Tim slipped up to my back. He must have taken a deep breath because he brushed my cheek and blew a bunch of air under my hat and in my ear.

I yelled to high heaven, punched Tim in the nose, squeezed the bucket flat between my legs, the cow kicked me on the leg and ran off – all at the same moment. As soon as I decided some kind of a wild animal wasn't trying to eat me alive I thought it was funny but that first scare was sure complete.

I was always a little spooky after night anyway and it sure worked perfect for Tim.

Another time I guess he decided to sort milk cows. Again he was the overnight horse. We always had a lot of bells on the cows. I woke up just as it was day light and could hear the bells moving around at the corral. The sound was real sharp and I could tell quite a few cows were moving around. I thought a gate had come open somewhere and the cows were leaving.

I walked partway to the barn and couldn't see any cows leaving. I guess Tim had got bored with nothing to do so decided to sort cows. He would get one and drive her across the corral and leave her in the corner. Go to the bunch, get another, and repeat the process. Finally he put all of the rest in the corner. He finished by driving them all back to the corner where he started and walked away. The cows didn't mind or get upset as they were gentle anyway but it really was quite a sight to see him work with no one around.

I don't suppose he was any smarter than any other horse but it seemed so to me as he was my favorite at that time.

I left the ranch the spring of '48 and left him there. He got hurt some way during the '49 blizzard, didn't recover and they had to let him go.

A Chicken Story

SPEAKING OF THE CHICKENS, we had an old hen. She was every color known to man. If she had been a horse she would have been a true Appaloosa. Every year just before winter she would hide out in her nest. About the first snow she would come out of the brush with six or eight little chickens. Dad always let her in the barn for a few days before taking her to the chicken house.

That old hen, though small, was tough. She would immediately clean that end of the barn of all livestock. Dogs, cats, kids, and anything that moved, left her end of the barn alone. Cows and horses were especially hated. The little chicks always did O.K. and we would think of having them for Christmas dinner but never did. Some of her offspring were around for years.

THE XV OR ARNOLD CORPORATION

WILL JUST SLIP IN a couple of items not about our horses.

The first year that the XV or Arnold Corporation rented the Forest Reserve they hadn't had time to set up a camp and Dad rode for them until they had one set up.

I was six or seven and when he was just checking mills and water on the closer pastures he let me ride along. The days seemed to get a little long but we rode pretty slow and took a lunch along. I always raised a lot of hell if he left me home. Probably needed shook but he took me whenever he could.

They hadn't cut him much for horse power. He figured just a bunch of junk no one else wanted to ride. A couple were bucking horses and the rest either sore backs or too old to use. He usually rides his own horses if he had some hard riding to do.

One morning he took one of the horses that wanted to buck. He had me ride Trix as a lead horse and go across the river in front of him so the Arnold horse would follow. We got across the river and nearly to the bank. In fact Trix and I were up on the bank. The water was about a foot deep and had a little current when the Arnold horse came unglued. Now that's a feeling you don't get anywhere else in the world. You can tell your horse is bucking but the running water, the sky, and your balance all run together and you're plumb out of kilter.

Actually Dad was putting up a plumb good ride but said as dizzy as he was getting he would just step off and save getting bucked off and wet all over. It didn't work. He lost his balance and went out of sight in about a foot of water. Came up sputtering, mad, and soaked to the skin. He got back on and tried to wear out about ten feet of hard twist rope on the horse's rump. When he finally got his head up we rode to the house for dry clothes. Then back to the river again. There was another fight that Dad won and then went to work. The horse never pulled this again and turned out to be a good pick for an all day ride.

Another time that summer we were riding salt boxes out on the Steer Creek. Ran onto a stray and Dad wanted to rope him and pick the brand to see who he belonged to. The old grey horse he was riding played out before he could get the critter caught. We were in some big high sand hills so he left me and his horse on top of one so he could sure find us. He put his saddle on my horse and went on with the project. Came back and as we were changing saddles we hear a sharp clink sound. In looking around we found a little cow bell. It had been there so long the clapper was rusted out. We took it home and used it on our cows for years but we never could even guess how a cow bell happened to be clear on top of the highest sand hill in that Steer Creek pasture.

Late that summer Arnold's got a camp set up by a windmill. Just a sheep wagon for protection and a little jingle pasture to catch horses. Later they set up a permanent camp on Steer Creek.

They got a special permit that fall and the rider stayed there until away into winter and maybe all winter. Those sheep wagons aren't much to hold heat and the wind came through the floor pretty bad. They either lost a steer or butchered one so he took the hide and laid it flesh side down on the floor. Of course, it froze and when he moved out late in the winter he couldn't pull it out so he just rode off and left it. As I remember he had either quit or got fired and never came back.

That was probably a good thing as when anyone came back it was well into spring and turning summer. They smelled the wagon long before they got to it. Finally they got the door open. The hair was slipping on the hide and maggots and blow flies had taken over. It was so bad they just destroyed it and never used it again.

Some of those things sound weird now but I guess the human race was tougher then.

When my mother and dad were first married the mice got in the cracker box. They just set the box full of crackers on the floor in an extra room intending to throw it out later. They left for a day or so and the hired man got a couple of meals for himself. They asked him what he had eaten and he said "soup and crackers." Sure enough, the cracker box was empty.

The kerosene lamp seemed to draw small bugs by the millions. It was a constant battle to keep them out of the jelly, butter and syrup pitcher. Especially at supper time or just after dark. When Dad was riding for the XV they used to bring salt and other supplies out from Nenzel in a little truck. Wouldn't be much of a truck now but it was then. Probably could handle two ton of salt at the most.

A little dirty old man drove it and always came in just at supper time. That was alright as everyone fed everyone at meal time. Mom happened to be gone and Dad had been batching. He had some chokecherry jam that he had forgotten to take from the table. He hadn't moved it because it was absolutely solid with little knats.

The little trucker sat at the table and Dad went into the kitchen for the last of the supper. When he came back he discovered the old gent eating hell out of the jam, putting it on his bread. Dad told him he thought there was some knats in it and to wait a second and he would get him some different.

The trucker said he "lowed as how they jest tasted like jam" to him and kept on eating.

As I recall he lived well into his eighties, so there for your new fangled ideas about modern sanitation.

Poke Kidder and a Horse Named Fred

POKE KIDDER WAS A man raised out in those Sandhills about half way between Kilgore and Mullin. I mean that's out where there is just a whole lot of nothing. I have been a long ways down in those hills and never got to Poke's place.

I knew the Swanson outfit was close to him and asked Garrett Swanson if the things I had heard about Poke were true. I repeated what I had heard and Garrett assured me they were so.

He said no man ever had a better friend or worse enemy than Poke Kidder. He said the kids in the Kidder family were raised the toughest of any one in the Sandhills.

This was way back when the very first homesteads were established in Cherry County. It seems the dad just had a small homestead shanty on his claim. Hardly room for all of the family to get under cover so at night the boys all slept outside. They would just take a couple of quilts and bed down under a wagon or in a pile of hay if they happened to have one. They did this clear into winter with snow on the ground. Never undressed, just got up in the morning and went into breakfast.

Of course Poke had a given name but it seems he had a lot of freckles and they called him Polka Dot which was shortened to Poke in later years. He wore a full beard from the time he was a young man and was supposed to have said he had always been the goat so he just as well look like one.

Garrett said Poke was honest to a fault with his friends but could be just bad towards people he didn't like. These two families were close friends and Garrett said the Kidders were welcome to anything on their outfit.

Now it seems the big outfits had a way of putting a deeded ranch together in homestead days. This was when most of Cherry County was still open range. They would hire a crew of cowboys to work for them with the understanding they were to take a homestead close by. They would keep them on the payroll and feed them while they proved up on their claims, which at completion was a section of land. They would put a small shack on the land which made the homestead legal and no one ever came to check how much they stayed in them. They were never there at all. When they owned the land they would sell it to the big outfit for a hundred dollars or so and leave. Of course they didn't have any use for the land anyway as no one could make a living on a section of sand hills and the free range was getting fenced in.

Poke was involved some way as a cowboy. It seems when it was time for them to sell out, some way they sold to Poke instead of the big outfit and left the country.

That is how he became a land owner. He bought more land as more years went by but that was his start. The big outfit declared war on Poke but he was the toughest and was there long after the big outfit was gone.

One time they tried to trap him by bringing a few cattle unbranded thinking Poke would probably steal them and brand them for himself. They marked these cattle by making a small incision in the skin of the animal and slipping in a silver dime. Silver doesn't cause infection and the little cut would heal in a few days.

Sure enough the cattle came up missing and as Poke had some stuff freshly branded they got the law and went to check. They roped and checked a couple of them and sure enough the dimes were there. They accused Poke and he said just keep on roping as he always marked his cattle that way. They did and found dimes under the skin of most of his young stock. Of course he must have been tipped off by someone but it was never proved that Poke ever stole a head of cattle.

He had a fight with a neighbor who lived just under a hill close to Poke's south fence. The hill was quite high for a sand hill and not very big around. Poke fenced off the top of the sand hill and put down a well on the very top. He would put a bunch of cattle by the mill and leave them for a few days and then change cattle. He did this until the grass was gone and the hill turned to pure fine sand. In a short time he had created a twenty or so acre blow out. Of course, the fence blew out, the mill blew down. Poke moved his cattle but the blow out was there and day by day covered up the neighbor's house and buildings and he had to move his headquarters.

His friends always contended he was really easy to get along with if you talked a problem out but absolutely diabolical if he was crossed.

He was well up in years and had some sort of run in with a patrolman.

They sent him a letter to turn in his driver's license or they would come get it. I'm weak on where this happened but as he wouldn't turn it in they went after it in some manner and met Poke coming to town. They stopped him and said to come with them and walked up to the pickup. They found themselves looking at a big forty five and were informed that he was coming to town, would meet them in court when he got there, that the license was sold by the state and no pipsqueak could legally take it away. They went to court, he argued his own case on that basis and he walked out with his license.

He either read a lot or had a built in mind for legality because he was involved in a number of lawsuits when we lived there. He always argued his own case before the judge and usually won. I'm also sure this can happen easier in Cherry County than some other places.

Some time close to 1920 corn was a very good price. The old ranch had quite a lot of farm ground on it and for sand hill land would raise a pretty good crop if the seasons would break right.

Dad said they had raised a real good crop of corn that year and had a good supply on hand but sure didn't intend to sell any.

Poke Kidder needed a load of corn, about 30 bushels at that time but didn't have any money for awhile. A man by the name of Thompson told Poke he could get a load of corn from Galloway's on credit and came after it with a team and high wheeled wagon. Dad didn't know Poke but he knew Thompson and though they didn't want to sell the corn he let them have a load as they needed it so bad and had come so far after it. Personally, I bet it was turned into whiskey but that's just a guess.

It was a while before the corn was paid for but the money came with a thank you and an extra ten dollars.

So much for Poke and back to the bad side of a "double u" and how he was involved with a couple of horses from the old ranch.

Now these facts are my own as told to me by Poke himself and facts as I knew them myself.

I ran into Poke in a café in Valentine. He was well up in years but sure positive in his speech. I introduced myself and he immediately told me what fine people Galloway's were and how ugly mean their horses had been. He mentioned the corn and how glad he was to get it.

It seems he was short on horses and as this Thompson was working there he came to the old ranch to try to borrow a couple of young horses and they would break them to ride if they could use them for a year.

I think Uncle Charley Galloway let them have 2 in the deal. Whether they had ever been tried or not I don't know. Thompson led them back to Kidder's. One was named Fred which I remember well and I don't know anything about the other.

Poke told me they started to break them and they were two of the meanest bucking horses he had ever seen before or since. Actually they got the horses broke and they were sure all day horses and would work cattle good but they both bucked every time they were saddled and any time during the day. They would go all day and buck coming in at night. He said they were the only horses they had ever seen that they didn't break. It came haying time the next year and they offered to break them to work as they couldn't break them to ride. Galloway's told them to go ahead as they sure as hell weren't any good the way they were.

Now came the double u on these horses when they hooked them on a mowing machine. I imagine it was easy to over do the use of it as they were probably getting even for all of the times the horses had bucked with them. The horses learned real quick when they heard whoa to stop or be thrown down. Only thing was they learned too well. When they heard whoa they would freeze up and balk. They would stop, refuse to move, and if they were crowded, throw themselves.

Poke said they never got them broke in any manner and at the end of two years gave up and took them back to Galloway's.

Now I don't know about the other horse. Maybe they just killed him but the Fred horse could be worked if you were real careful. I remember Dad hooked him with Duke on a mower. He froze up, threw himself and Dad just left him lay there and harnessed another horse and went on with the mowing. Fred was still laying there when he came to dinner but stood up during the afternoon.

So it is possible to over use a double u and put too good a whoa on your horses.

Dad just turned Fred out, didn't use him at all and as he really was a good looking horse everyone wanted to either buy or trade for him, but didn't want to give any price at all. Dad decided people thought he was afraid of the horse so he got him in and by being careful worked him in the cornfield and during haying all one summer.

That fall they had the "Happy Day Picnic." This was a little local rodeo that had quite a lot of horse races with pretty good prize money for them and also the bronc and bareback riding. Everyone brought their horses that they knew or thought would buck to use in the contest.

Now odd as it seems even though Fred was hell to handle if he was crossed was gentle if he wasn't. Dad just tied him to Old Pal's saddle horn. I rode my saddle horse and led them to the picnic which was seven miles away with at least a half dozen gates to open. I was eight and boy was I in kid's heaven.

Plat Calvin drew Fred in the saddle broncs for that afternoon. He rode him alright and afterwards Dad asked if that horse was hard to ride. Plat told him that he might have ridden a few that were harder to ride but had never ridden one that hit the ground so hard. He said although he had been off for fifteen minutes he felt like his eyes were still crossed.

There was no arena. The horses came out of a breakaway chute and when the whistle blew the cowboys just hoped the pickup men could get to them and if they couldn't just bailed out any way they could. This was in a good sized pasture and sometimes the bronc riders didn't get their saddles back until the next day.

Would you believe they didn't judge time by a watch? The judges counted the jumps a horse made. I don't know how many jumps was a ride but then they had to spur the horse so many times ahead of the cinch and so many behind.

Dad had given me the halter for Fred as he was busy at some other job and wasn't mounted. I was to take the halter to the pickup man to put on Fred after the ride was over. He picked up with no problem but I couldn't get the pickup man's attention to take my halter and not turn Fred loose. His name was Pitzer and a real good man. Probably wondered what that damn kid was doing out there in the road yelling at him.

Fred just stood there looking at me and my horse. Dad walked out, took the halter and started to walk up to him. Dad was about ten feet away when Fred struck, he never moved his hind feet. Just reared a little and struck with both front ones. I can still hear those feet hit that ground and the dust just flew. Dad yelled the usual "Whoa Fred you S. of a B. Whoa."

Fred was true to his training and though his whoa'er was fixed too good he never moved another muscle. Just stood and Dad put on the halter and they walked away.

The next spring a horse buyer came through to pick up as big horses as he could find to send to the cotton fields. He gave Dad eighty bucks for Fred and never even asked for him to be driven. That was a real high price at that time and the horse was well up in years.

We still think a horse should have a whoa but they fixed the one on Fred too good and that is how it happened.

Dolly and a Floyd Jones Story

PROBABLY WAS ABOUT ELEVEN and owned a calf. I wanted a calf to break to ride and play with. The calf wasn't worth much to me. You couldn't ride them. They wouldn't multiply for a long time and to a kid the time it takes for a calf to have any value is forever.

The neighbors had a couple of colts and offered to trade me one for my calf. I'm sure he knew Dad wouldn't let me trade but I was all for the deal.

At that time the Forest service let us know free grazing on the forest as it wasn't very well watered and they had trouble getting enough cattle in the summer time to even start to keep the grass down.

We probably had fifteen or twenty horses out there and though they were pretty well bred were mostly old mares and cripples and had no value. This was in the winter time and the old mares had had four or five colts on them born that spring.

Dad and I held a little horse roundup on a nice winter day and he gave me a nice bay mare colt out of the bunch, probably to keep me quiet, with the understanding I was to take full care of her and if I didn't she went back to the wild bunch.

She broke to lead real easy and the rest of the winter was kept in the barn in beside my saddle horse I rode to school. She really was a little doll, a sweet little mare, and by spring I was riding her around the yard and she just came along fine.

The next winter she had to spend out on the range but at spring roundup she came in nice and fat so I put her in the jingle pasture to use the next morning to wrangle horses.

She was real gentle and I could catch her anywhere. I took my bridle and jumped on her bareback. She walked away real nice and then I made another of the mistakes I seemed to be addicted to. I thought it would be fun to lope in to the corral so I kicked her in the belly.

I found out real quick how big a mistake that can be. The first jump I came down straddle of her neck just behind her ears and for just a moment I thought I might get a handful of ears and somehow ride out the storm. The second jump I was upside down and ironed out on the ground. She had stopped but I sure didn't. I turned clear over, came down flat on my back in cactus as usual. I rode her on to the barn but was very careful not to offend her.

Anyway, I learned the hard way to don't ride bareback unless you are very very careful. Or did that mare just wait to give me a hard lesson? Believe me, if you live with horses you will learn a lot.

Late the same summer I was at the corral and had just pulled my cinch tight. Mom called from the house and said there was no hurry. I jumped on Doll and made that famous mistake again. I kicked her in the belly and got horse back real suddenly. Thanks to a high horned saddle, which I sure had both hands on, I managed to stay up till the storm was over.

She turned into a real nice saddle horse and did the ranch a lot of good. I rode her back and forth on weekends when I was going to high school in Kilgore. That was the only two times she ever bucked and was so handy because you could catch her anywhere anytime. I lost her in later years because I wanted a colt of hers so bad and she had trouble.

So as I always say – I was young enough I don't feel I taught Doll anything but she sure taught me real sharp. Don't jump on quick and kick them in the belly. To this day I still saddle up, turn them around a couple of times, step up and very gently ask them to walk away, please. Those sudden starts won't work.

***** This is another story and quite a few years later but it fits so well with what Doll taught me, will slip it in.

Floyd Jones Story

THE XV OR ARNOLD Corporation had a camp on the Forest Reserve and Floyd Jones was boss. They were a big outfit north of Cody and had hundreds of cattle on the forest. Floyd would move to the camp at fencing time, in the spring, and stay until the pastures were rounded up in the fall, usually in November.

They hauled his grub to him and he only came out a couple of times during that time. They did have one of the old one-line telephones but unless he needed some extra help on windmills, or some special job, he was alone.

When he needed help he would hire some of us along the river. This happened when DDT first came out. It was supposed to kill all lice and flies on cattle so they would make a better weight gain. I don't know if it did or not but the XV decided to round up all their cattle and spray them. The brought in a crew from the main ranch but Jones also hired me for a few days and the job was sure welcome. I was grown by this time but sure needed the extra bucks. He told me to bring my own horses as he didn't know how many they would send from the main ranch and we might run short.

As it turned out they brought a crew, a cook, and about 75 head of horses. I got in there about midnight. It was real dark, so I turned my horses loose, unsaddled at the camp shack, found a bedroll and went to sleep.

The next morning at 3:30, and I mean 3:30, Jones yelled, "Hey you damn Mexicans. Get a shovel and start digging." I don't know what that was supposed to mean but it started the day. By the time we finished breakfast the wrangler was in with the horses and Billy Pourier was roping whatever horses the men called for. I asked Jones what horse to take and I told Billy. He roped a darn good looking bay. The horse was tall, solid, and sure looked to have a lot of miles in him. He also had a snort you could hear a half a mile and enough white in his eyes to start a snow storm.

I got a little suspicious because Jones had told me this was supposed to be a horse out of his string that he rode all the time. Jones had been a hell of a bronc rider in his day but had gotten older and quit.

I walked down the rope and the horse never moved a foot. Just kept snorting, rolling his eyes and sort of starting to sit down. I had visions of him coming back up in the middle of me. Believe me, right then I wished I was back on the Niobrara River with my milk cows.

He let me bridle him with no problem and I noticed those guys watching pretty close as I led him up to my saddle. Lucky for me my saddle was away from them.

Just as I finished saddling Jones came out of the cook shack and asked what in hell I was doing with that horse. I told him Bill caught him for me. He said, "That S.O.B. at you. That horse has bucked off every man out there but I think you can fool hell out of them. Your horses don't buck and as good as your saddle fits a horse, here's what you do. Leave that cinch loose about a quarter of an inch from his belly. Turn him around three or four times, slip up easy but don't hesitate, and get out of here before those S.O.B.'s get to you."

Believe me I did just that because if that old boy had come unglued I couldn't have ridden one side of him. He probably knew it and so did I. Maybe that's what saved me. He walked off pretty as a picture. I got to a big sand blowout, got him in a trail, then a lope and three miles west and three miles back. He was pretty well winded and I met the rest of the crew.

I rode him all morning and after dinner when they tried to get me to change horses as they were doing I just said, "Nope, if I have to break these horses I'm just going to stay up here and finish the job."

I used that horse all through the job. Took him home with me, as I was short on horse power. I used him to wrangle with, trotted hound pups behind him, Alice even rode him a few times.

He was an all day horse and never did even offer to buck. After a couple of months I didn't need him anymore as I had three or four colts going good. I took him back to Jones. They kept him in that night to wrangle horses the next morning and he bucked the wrangler off before he was out of the corral.

I'm sure this story had a happy ending for me just because I learned from Jones how to saddle him and Doll taught me not to kick her in the belly.

Digging Potatoes

ONE YEAR THE POTATO crop around home was real poor and during the winter spuds got up pretty high and in the spring price of seed potatoes was high. As your garden spots were all sub-irrigated along the river we had plenty and sold a few to the neighbors for seed.

We had a few bushels left over so I plowed up a big spot at the Rauer place and as I could get my hands on a potato planter put it into spuds, hoping to have a chance to sell a bunch in the fall. It was pretty late in June but the crop really came on even though it was only cultivated one time.

I had never checked them so one rainy cold day in September I took a pitch fork, team, and high wheeled two box wagon and went across the river to check my spud crop. It was absolutely unbelievable. I have never seen a better crop before or since. I suppose I dug 8 or 10 bushel in just a little while and started home. I hadn't expected to get so many so easy so I hadn't put in the back end gate on the wagon box. Didn't think it would make much difference as the potatoes would lay pretty well and if I lost a few it wouldn't matter anyway with a crop like I'd found there.

Always had a bunch of dogs around and that day there were 3 coyote hounds and a couple of shepherds along. Started home and the team I was driving were pretty good travelers. They were pretty dumb and you had to drive them constantly so we only used them when we had to. They could really run and would run away if they got a chance. We never worried about it much if we had a hold on the lines because you could always drive them and you just got home quicker.

Just got started home good when an old coyote rolled out of the brush and started up a long slope toward the rim rocks. The dogs took the coyote, the horses took the dogs, and me, and the spuds went along for the ride. I noticed by going up a slope my spuds were jumping out the back of the wagon box. I sort of stood in the middle to try and hold them in but they sure had to take second place to my attention to a coyote chase.

Now we had traveled about ¼ mile when the dogs went out of sight but sure grabbing at the coyote. When the horses and I got to that spot they were pretty well winded and the dogs were out of sight. We started down along the slope getting their wind and me kicking spuds to the front of the wagon box.

We got to the bottom of the slope into a canyon and here came the dogs back to the wagon in high gear with the coyote chasing them.

The coyote saw me and stopped. The dogs saw they had some help and away we went again up another slope. Coyote, dogs, wagon and me. At the top of that slope we all gave up. Coyote went on into the brush. The dogs came to me, the horses got their wind back so we started home. Got in about dark, did a few chores and took my potatoes to the house. Everyone agreed they were such nice big potatoes, all twelve quarts of them.

Everyone in the country raised a good spud crop. I couldn't give away or sell any of them and the coyote wouldn't have been worth picking up if they had caught it.

I imagine it was an old female who lit up away from her pups but at least I still had plenty of potatoes and one hell of a coyote chase.

Coyote Hunting Tales

It was snowing light one evening,
To a party we were bound
Away out in the sandhills
'Bout 50 miles from town.
The talk just kinda roamed around
Till a certain subject tumbled,
From that time on the talk flew fast
And that ranch house fairly rumbled.

About September 17th
The end of Indian summer
The coyote seasons getting close
And sure to be a hummer.
So say a bunch of ranchers
And cowboys who should know
Who are gathered for the evening
At a ranch called C Bar O.

So the conversation quickly turns
To coyotes tricks and hounds,
Each guy has his story,
And this is how it sounds.
Now Old Spot was the fastest dog
And when it came to fight,
He'll kill that doggone coyote
Or he won't be home tonight.

So says old Pete of the Bar Bar D
Bill Jones picks up the tale
Well boys I had a hound dog once
And boy he sure could trail.
He'd hit them in the sandhills
Then he'd trail them to the flat
Then it sure was goodnight coyote
Cause he'd wipe them off the map.

Next comes Chuck Lead's story
He's got some hound dogs too
They might not be the fastest
But they're all the way true blue.
Now Jonny Simms he gets a chance
And grabs the conversation
And tells of all the bushy tails,
And his dogs on the reservation.

So minutes fly and hours slip
And finally one by one
Each feller tells his little tale
Of what his dogs have done.
Some don't seem quite possible,
And others could be true,
But each guy had the better dog,
As everyone could prove.

At 2 o'clock the party breaks,
And everyone heads home
A dreaming dogs and coyotes,
And chases sure to come.
Of coyotes caught and chased and lost
And horses who could follow
A snarly up a slipping hill
And catch him in the hollow.

Now if those dogs were in one pack
Chasin' coyotes for a bounty
There wouldn't be a wooly left
In the hills of Cherry County.
But I wouldn't trade one evening
Of cowboys and their chases
For a dozen city parties
With all their pretty faces.

Jack and Nancy and one of Jack's hunting dogs

That Old Saddle

By Martin Bergin

Ya' see that old saddle
    up there on the rack
By far the oldest
    in a room full of tack.

In years it must be
    a 100 or so
Fer it belonged to a good puncher
    back long years ago.

You say what's its value
    in dollars today
Hell, you'd have to pay
    someone to pack it away.

But it's worth more than money
    to me don't you see
For it belonged to my grandpaw
    who left it to me.

Reprinted with permission from Martin Bergin

*Jack's Great-Grandson Ketch Rope Hamar with the Hamley Saddle. Ketch is
the only son of Marty Hamar, Nancy's son*

SADDLE CERTIFICATE OF AUTHENTICITY

Since 1883, Hamley's has produced some of the finest in saddles and hand crafted leather goods. The following information has been authenticated from the original saddle records of Hamley and Company, Pendleton, Oregon and is as complete as available.

Serial number: C295 J706
Made by: Leonard Nichols
Made for: Jack J. Galloway, Kilgore, Nebraska
Date: May 15, 1943   Original Price: $128.98

_____   1-13-11
Signature   Date

30 SE Court Pendleton, OR 97801
541-278-1100 www.hamley.com

May 15, 1943

Jack J. Galloway
Kilgore, Nebraska

Parcel Post

B635

```
#C295 Saddle, Serial No. J706          94.50
 California Round Skirts                2.00
#57L 1½" Stirrups                       2.45
                                       ‾‾‾‾‾
                                       98.95
       10% Inc. as of 7/1/41            9.90
1 pr. #104 Saddle Pockets, stamped as
                    saddle             15.13
 New Stirrup Leather Feature            5.00
                                      ‾‾‾‾‾‾
                                      128.98
1 Navajo #43607                        13.50
35 ft. #1 Silk Giant Rope               1.93
                                      ‾‾‾‾‾‾
                                      144.41
       Postage & C.O.D. Fee             3.06
                                      ‾‾‾‾‾‾
                                      147.47
       By Cash                         50.00
       Balance C.O.D.                  97.47
```

College Classes

J ACK ATTENDED COLLEGE FOR a time at Chadron, Neb., and he wasn't too happy there. He could write poems about teachers they couldn't satisfy and what a waste more education was to him. He wanted to go home to the ranch.

What's Wrong with Our Brains

We write them in History, it surely is tough,
We may write 20 pages, but that's not enough.
We don't indent right, we misspell our words.
Our grammar is always the worst, the worst that you've heard.

Our themes are on Johnson, Jackson and Grant.
We try to do right, but just simply can't.
For months we've been working, and trying in vain,
But now we decide, something's wrong with our brain.

English Lit

We have many subjects,
From which we may pick
I made a mistake
It sure makes me sick.

I don't like the damn stuff
But still I must sit,
Through 45 minutes
Of English Lit.

Jack at College

Armistice Day ---and Night

The following poem was written while Jack was attending Chadron College

There's one night I am quite certain,
That I never will forget.
'Twas the eleventh of November,
When Chadron was so wet.
Our football team took Kearney.
And it wasn't very late.
When Saskey, Brown, and Ballard,
Thought they'd ought to celebrate.

They made their way right to the bar,
And not once did they lag,
Believe you me by supper time.
Those boys were "in the bag."
They ate their supper all at once,
And then with steps unsteady,
They wandered back up to their room,
Until the dance was ready.

They sallied forth upon the street,
In Saskey's new V8,
They had to have a few more beers,
Before it was too late.
Here Saskey quit the party,
He simply had to go.
But how he wandered home that night,
I'm sure we'll never know.

The dance hall drew their interest,
And here when they are seen,
There's a dance or two ahead of them,
And a drink or two between.
All too soon the dance was over,
So in the Pullman they did sit,
To drink a cup of coffee,
And to kid the girls a bit.

At three o'clock they started home.
But no matter how they'd try,
They simply had to turn aside,
To let the posts go by.
Finally they both made it home,
And tumbled into bed,
To sleep the few remaining hours,
And snore to wake the dead.

The boys awoke next morning,
With eyes bloodshot and sore,
With their pocketbooks quite empty,
And clothes upon the floor.
They say they won't get drunk again.
But I have got a hunch,
That they are only waiting,
Till their paycheck comes next month.

THE LIVES OF GREAT MEN

Lives of great men, all remind us,
We can make our lives sublime,
And departing leave behind us,
Footprints in the sands of time.

Lives of great men all remind us,
Of the things we hope to get,
But how to keep it once it's gotten,
No one seems to've found out yet.

We have many subjects,
From which we may pick,
I made a mistake,
It sure makes me sick.
I don't like the dern stuff
But still I must sit,
Through 45 minutes of English Lit.

You read about Shakespeare,
And Chaucer and Steele,
Goldsmith and Collins,
Till sometimes you feel,
Like you'll die if you ever,
Must take one more look,
Or hunt up a name,
In that old English book.

There's dozens of poets,
And prose writers, too,
We study them all,
But when we are through,
We forget what we've read,
"Cause we all wondered how,
These fellas would look,
Writing poetry now.

Tough Luck

There's a night in my life,
I'll never forget,
I fell in the creek,
And got rather wet.
I'll explain to you now,
How this came about,
For baths in a creek
I can sure do without.

We had gone on a picnic
Sometime after dark.
And all of us thought
It would be quite a lark.
We soon built a fire,
Out there in the trees,
With everyone laughing
As gay as you please.

But disaster soon came,
And I cannot see,
Of all who were there,
It had to hit me.
We boys who were trying
To be gallant and strong,
Were hunting green sticks
To roast marshmallows on.
I found a big patch
Of chokecherry brush

So naturally I
Began with a rush
To break off the branches
For all I was worth
When blooie the bottom
Dropped out of the earth.

I went down like a shot,
Now laugh if you please,
And lit in some water,
Clear up to my knees.
I yelled for some help,
Believe it or not,
Because in September
The water's not hot.

Three husky fellows
Soon gave me a hand,
And hoisted me up
Again to dry land.
But I still insist
With never a doubt,
These baths in a creek,
I can sure do without.

It's two o'clock now,
And I should be in bed.
But I'm sitting here,
With a cold in my head.
If there's ever a time,
You want to get sick,
Just take my advice,
And fall in the creek.

Silly? Yes? Well, maybe ---

When a feller gets downhearted,
And no matter how he tries,
He feels he's doing right by no one,
And is tired of living lies,
Tho he tries to raise his spirits,
He knows it can't be done,
He don't want to be a coward,
So he musn't turn and run.

With three high school years behind him,
Money spent and nothing gained,
Knows the future's holding nothing,
Unless they know you're "trained."
You don't want to hurt your parents,
Who have hopes in store for you,
So you look into the future,
Wonder what you're going to do.

Gone the hope of being someone,
You feel completely lost
You're tired of books and schooling,
And always being bossed.
So now you stop and wonder,
If you haven't been a fool,
Wish you'd stayed at home with parents,
And never seen a school.

If you'd stayed at home and labored,
Early morning late at night,
You at least would have the feeling,
That you were doing right.
But with grades below the average,
You can't sleep half the night,
That's when you stop and wonder
If you're really doing right.

I wish I'd never seen a high school,
After all what good's it done,
I feel sorry for my parents,
'Cause they had me for a son,
Oh I know this all is silly,
Please forget and understand,
That a feller stopped and wrote this,
When he didn't give a damn.

I don't regret the last few years,
That came so quick and now are gone,
But I have to face a future,
That goes on and on and on,
You feel that you are worthless,
You feel all sad and blue,
When you look into the future,
And wonder what you're going to do.

Daddy Misses His Girls

Daddy misses his girls tonight
The house is empty and still
You should be home tomorrow
But I don't know if you will
Daddy missed his girls this morning
He missed them more at noon
Now it's almost bedtime
Won't you both come back home soon?

I know my girls are naughty
They don't do the things they
    should
But I'm the guy who spoiled
    them
As people knew I would.
They nearly drive me crazy
From morning until night
When Daddy kissed them both
    to bed
And put out all the lights.

Jack and Nancy

My girls are really sweethearts
I sure am lonesome tonight
Without my pair of little girls
It doesn't seem just right,
My little girl is 4 years old
And golly how I love her
I love my 22 year old,
My 4 year olds own mother.

Daughter Nicki at home on the ranch

ALICE

My Greatest Sacrifice

In the Sandhills we raise horses,
And you hear a lot of blarney
About our hotblood Thoroughbreds
That we sell to the Army.

The Army bought my horse once,
And I'm here to relate,
How I happen to be living
In the good old marriage state.

I broke this colt one summer,
He turned out plenty hot.
Some guys said the Army's
Probably buy him like as not.

You see, I had a girl friend,
And boy, she was a honey,
We wanted to get married,
But we didn't have no money.

So after lots of study,
And some feelings of remorse,
I went and let the Army,
See my good old cuttin' horse.

He passed without a question,
I put money in my pants,
Bought a marriage license
And gave a wedding dance.

So that's just how it happened,
I gave married life a whirl,
The Army's got my cuttin' horse,
But I've still got my girl.

I hope that she appreciates
And remembers all her life,
The sacrifice I had to make,
My top horse for a wife.

POEM FROM ALICE TO JACK

It was not often Alice tried her hand at poetry, she left that to Jack. It was written in 1949 because she mentions he's 30 that day. It was a heartfelt message to him from her.

From your wife and daughters we say
Best Wishes to Daddy on your birthday.
We love you a lot, for being just you.
Believe us for these words are so true.

We'll say them often as the years go by
Because you are you, that is why.
The very best husband a woman ever had
And to Nancy and Nicki the very best Dad.

Please don't laugh at our literary style
It comes from my heart, so please just smile.
Thirty today and to me not old
You say the things I like to be told.

We're not trying to write a good poem
Just writing of the guy who makes any place home.
Just writing of how very much we love you
The guy who's Dad to my daughters, two.

The husband I love so very much
And the Daddy who has the loving touch.
The guy who never complains when failures I bake
The one who is there when the girls' legs ache.

We'll sing his praises up to the sky
The nicest husband, the very best guy.
He's thirty years old on this very day,
The guy I'm writing about in my poor way.

Just common place things of every day life.
So very wonderful to his daughters and wife.
We can't give you presents that cost a lot of money,
Just tell you and show you we love you, honey.

So please don't worry about giving us a big palace.
We just love you – signed All yours, Alice

Alice on Princess

More Butterfly and Alice

THEY SAY TO WRITE you have to have something to write about. I'm afraid I have so many of these I'll never get them all written.

Yes – don't get horses afraid. Alice and I were on the Rauer place on the south side of the river. On the north side was hay meadow. Between the meadow and high dry ground is a swamp, filled with rushes, bogs, etc. At the west end the gooey mud is quite thin with only an inch or so of water on top and as far as we knew, and even know yet, it is bottomless. Through the years a lot of cattle and quite a few weak horses have drowned in this bog hole and we avoided it.

Again, we were short on horses and as Butterfly was gentle by that time I had Alice riding her and they both were very pregnant.

Our milk cows and a few others had got out of our pasture and were grazing around the north side of this boggy ground. I was coming home with a load of corn and Alice on Butterfly was following me. She was picking up the cattle and they were coming around the west end of the swamp. I expected her to follow them and stay on hard dry ground, but she didn't.

I went across the river with the corn, stopped to unhook at the barn. The cows came in with Alice behind them. She came on to get unsaddled and I nearly fainted. That mare was covered with mud clear up to her neck, up the saddle swells and over her tail. Alice had mud up over her knees. She said it was shorter to ride across the swamp and as all the cows were coming she had just cut across.

I'm sure Butterfly had to have swam a little of the muck. I'm also sure you could not have put a cowboy in that spot with a gun or get anyone to this day to bet they could cross that spot. Alice wasn't scared. Butterfly wasn't scared so they made it all right. Only one afraid was me, and that was afterwards.

You all have seen the cartoon of the horse jumping off the cliff with the old cowboy pulling the reins and yelling "Whoa you S.O. B. Whoa."

How many times I have yelled the same thing. Sometimes it works. Sometimes it don't, but we learned pretty young that the first thing to fix on your horse is the "Whoa."

Although I haven't thought much about it I guess I had fixed the "Whoa-er" on Butterfly pretty well. As I have mentioned before, after she was raising colts and running with the brood mares we would sometimes stick her in a chute with just a halter on her head. Open the gate, stick your spurs in her shoulders and she never failed to put on a darn good show. Pick her up, stick a bridle on and any little girl could ride her away.

We were having a little fun rodeo there at the ranch and had a lot of fun races like spud races, bundle races, husband and wife rescue races, etc.

We had bucked out a lot of cows and started on a few horses. There were a couple of pretty good cowboys there and they put on a good show. A young fellow was there and willing to get on something but of course didn't want anything too rough as he was just starting. He wasn't afraid so I gave him Butterfly.

We got him set in the box and I reminded him to be sure to spur her when the gate opened. He didn't forget and instead of going for her shoulders his spurs just hit her belly - kerthunk.

Believe me it made the old girl mad and she even bellered. Made a couple of high, sort of twisting jumps and bucked him out of his saddle and straight ahead. I suppose when she felt him go she thought she was through and put her head up, just in time to catch him coming down. He lit ahead of his saddle and straddle of her neck. Nothing between him and the ground but her ears. He yelled "Whoa." The old mare stopped and watched him crawl back in the saddle and walked away.

Yes – Fix their whoa-er is good advice.

Alice's Advice on Cowboys to Girls

And Jack's Questions

Alice told a young woman:
I remember once you told me
You had made it to the chutes
That you sure admired those cowboys
And you thought they were so cute.

You told me they were gentlemen
They sure lit up your life
Removed their hats and smiled at you
You thought they were so nice.

She said they were deceitful
Under handed, to move faster
They sure as hell would lie a lot
To get what they were after.

She said they never change a bit
From spring until the fall
But if she had to tell the truth
By gosh she loved them all.

Jack wonders:

I'm sure that this is good advice
But I am asking you
If she's qualified to give it
How the hell she knew.

She seems to have the answers
Of all you want to know
How she got her information
Just never seemed to show.

So if she should see some cowboys
And it seems to strike a spark
I'll go along and watch her
And listen in real sharp.
If she has found out all these facts
It really didn't show
I'll go along with her to find
The things that I don't know.

A Valentine for Alice

For just awhile things were a mess
I tried to send this Pony Express
Now your old mare is sure a fox
She wouldn't get in the damn mail box.

Outside of that things are just fine
If you'll please be my Valentine
Cause I'll tell you it'll come apart
If I must find a new sweetheart.

I know I'd look till I was through
And not find one as nice as you
So please pay heed to what's above
And wear this gift with lots of love.

Jack's poems to Alice

My Lady

Now men are alike
Most each day and night
Some things they do are sure shady
Whatever you think
You'll never wear mink
But you sure will wind up
    MY LADY

I'm Here to Stay

I simply cannot understand
It's what folks do to their fellow man
It's simply smile and bow and say hello
But God I'm glad to see you go.

So please believe why I love you
If there's a bump you'll see it through
I love you much I'm here to tell
I understand plain "Go to Hell."

I can't help it if I'm dumb
Hang around and I'll change some
Other folks can go away
I tell you gal, I'M here to stay.

Happy Birthday

I didn't stop to find a card
So I'll just stop and say
I hope you have 'bout 50 more
Returns of this one day.
Love, Jack

Happy St. Patrick's Day

They tell us of the luck of the Irish,
I know the stories are true,
And I am at the top of the whole damn pile,
Cause, baby, I got you.

Halloween

I like you, I think you're sweet,
Since this is the day for trick-or-treat
So you won't have me in a fix
Here's your treat, 'cause I need no tricks.

After Buying Another Horse

Some days are long
Some nights are dark
Some times are filled with ice
I brought you home this brood mare
Just because I think you're nice.

What is a Woman Thinking?

Here stands a man
Who can't understand
The facts of a lady's behavior,
She's sugar and spice
And everything nice
Makes evenings that I have to savor.

But the thing that bugs me
And I cannot see
With all of the time I spend drinking,
Is how in the hell
A poor man can tell
What on earth a woman is thinking?

What's Mine is Yours

I took your pickup
Don't be miffed
'Cause on the floor
You'll find a fifth.

Forever more
Just keep in mind
What's mine is yours
And yours is mine.

Taking Alice a Present

You've been so nice, you've been so good.
You've been so very pleasant
So I have finally figured out
You're looking for a present.

So please don't change your attitude.
With you I'm really smitten.
If you stay really nice to me,
I'll let you have this kitten.

Mother's Day Race

I'm sittin' here at the old race track
And tho I tried real hard
I simply didn't find the time
To hunt you up a card.

Tomorrow they say is Mother's Day
And you're both front and center
You're bound to place in any race
I decide for you to enter.

You sure can't go for a mile or so
Those nags are long and lean
You shape up more like a quarter horse
Your lines are round and clean.

So after giving it lots of thought
I'll leave it up to the weather
And you're bound to pull up 1st
If we get it all together.

The weatherman says it has to rain
So tomorrow you're going in
This is sure one race that you won't lose
Our money's on you to win.

We'll put it all on your pug nose
And forget about any other
You'll win this race just pulling away
'Cause you're sure one hell of a "Mudder."

Trying to Tempt His Lady

When it is handy then candy is dandy,
I'm sure that liquor is quicker,
But the girl that I doubt
And can't do without
Will look at the liquor and snicker.

Be My Valentine

I think you're neat
I think you're sweet
I think that you're just dandy
And tho you never drink my booze
I'll try you on some candy.

I try to figure best I can
I get what I am after
I guess you have me figured out
You always figure faster.

So even tho you are so smart
I'm going to win this time
'Cause all I'm going to ask you
Is to be My Valentine.
Love You

A Last Drink
Here's to the man
With a quart in his hand
And here's to the man who can think
But the man worth while
Is the one who can smile
When he leaves you his last drink.

Fears of the Beauty Parlor
I will stay here stay full of good cheer
I'll see that I'm full of pure ardor
For God's sake don't go and proceed to show
This note in your Beauty Parlor.

Reading My Mind
I never go high, but this I will bet
On this Monday evening you thought I'd forget.
But if you look around, I bet you will find,
I've got twenty bucks you are reading my mind.

I Love You
I love you when you're good and bad
I love you when you're mean
I love you in the morning light
And all times in between

But when I love you most of all
Regardless what you think
Is when you meet me at the bar
To buy Grandad a drink.

Who Needs a Harem?

Some guys have wives
They hate all their lives
Some also have wives who can scare 'em
But the way that we date
When you're feeling great
What in hell would I do with a harem?

A True Modern Lady

You're a true modern lady
A joy to behold
When the LORD created you
He busted the mold.

You bring home your paycheck
You have a big smile.
But I have some advice
You can think on awhile.

You keep the wolf from the door,
His tail, hair and hide.
Thank God you don't know
That he's waiting inside.

So if your job should fold up
Your bank account gone,
And you're needing some bucks
'Cause things have gone wrong.

Remember these words!
You have plenty of class
And if everything fails
You can peddle your BICYCLE.

It's cheaper than the damn FORD!

The End
Some folks act so awfully odd
You think you hardly know 'em
Tonight I'm in a hurry
So you don't get any poem!

When the construction season on Highway 20 was over in 1948, Jack went to work on the Junior Morris spread, a ranch south of Wood Lake. Apparently they got kind of lonesome because he wrote this letter to cousins during that time. Oh yes, he referred to Alice as his "big fat wife" and she wasn't five feet tall and about 110 pounds. That reference was all in fun.

Jack worked on this ranch when the Blizzard of 1949 hit. The ranch was snowed in for 30 days and he fed cows with work horses pulling a hay sled. The main ranch house had a telephone and they could call in orders to town so mail and groceries were dropped by airplane and school was closed. Snow was drifted over the gate post on the yard, which was probably seven feet high. When the road was finally bladed open, the family got to make a trip to Wood Lake for the first time in a month.

LETTER TO THE COUSINS

At breakfast this morning my big fat wife cried
Nobody writes, you would think they had died
There's Margaret and Walter and Darlene and Ted
From the letters I get you would think they were dead.

So drop us a line if you all love your cousin
We wouldn't care if we got a whole dozen
But if you have croaked in these fleeting hours
Just drop us a line and we'll send you some flowers.

We've been on the ranch one month to the day
We've plenty of work and not very much pay
We've plenty to eat but nothing to drink
But just the well water that runs in the sink.

It's been mighty cold you very well know
Plenty of wind, but not very much snow
We're not feeding much, just plenty of cake
If the wells all freeze up they can drink in the lake.

We have a new truck with a heater and such
So caking the cows just isn't so much
We have a new tractor to hook on our sled
Than harness a horse we would rather be dead.

We don't have much hay just windrows and range
Get by pretty good if the weather don't change
But boy if it snows and the drifts get up tall
Our Lone 90 stock will look pretty small.

My horse is just fine, he's fatter then jelly
Gets gallons of oats and hay to his belly
We've been pretty busy just fixing a shed
It's got a tin roof and the sides are all red.

We're milking 4 cows and we have plenty of cream
Just yesterday evening I really did scream
Another came fresh, she's sure not my dish
Her bag's like a tub and her tits like a fish.

Mommie gets fatter and Daddy does too
We're all pretty happy, no one's ever blue
The kids are just fine this evening because
In about one more month they'll see Santa Claus.

What happened to Jones? He owes us a letter
And answer he will, or at least he had better
Have you heard any scandal? Was anyone shot?
How about some strip poker when weather gets hot?

I've nothing to write but plenty to say
So hop in your car and come down some day
But remember my words, the thought you may hold
I'll play no strip poker, the weather's too cold.

It's 10 o'clock now, and I must hit the hay
'Cause 5 in the morning begins a new day
So write us a note whenever you can
As long as you're well why we don't give a damn.

We're sending our love to you and the kids
Drop us a line and don't tell any fibs
We have been there before and we're going to come back
To see you again so lots of love

                    Jack

Jack took his family and moved to O'Neill in 1949 to learn to be a lineman for Consumer's Public Power. This was in the days before bucket trucks and safer ways of servicing the high wires. He wrote this poem during that time.

YOUR LINEMAN

Who took his job as a plumb green kid
Who didn't care just what he did
He lived and learned of high wire lines
And could have quit ten thousand times.
　　Your lineman

Who dug the holes and took the brunt
When everybody called him grunt
Who crawled a pole and took a chance
Then hit the ground on the seat of his pants.
　　Your lineman

Who learned to watch and work and play
So he could live another day
Who felt damn small as the days rolled by
But always gave it another try.
　　Your lineman

Who finally earned the right to climb
And do that work on the high hot line
Who knows he's good cause he has to be
His work's right there for all to see.
　　Your lineman

Who learned his job and is kind of mean
And sometimes snarls at a kid that's green
Who learned it well to use his head
The right mistake and he's a long time dead.
　　Your lineman

When lightning strikes or the blizzards moan
Who sits right close to the telephone
Who sleeps with his boots beside his bed
When the lights go out and the lines go dead.
    Your lineman

When trouble comes who's on his way
On cold dark nights or light of day
Who knows his job won't be much fun
But lights are out and it must be done.
    Your lineman

So remember this and give kind looks
To the guy you see in belts and hooks
And remember please and remember well
He's had good times
And lots of hell.
    Your lineman

Jack was a member of the Meadville Roping Club when he lived in Ainsworth. Club members would travel to other clubs for a "match roping" where scores were kept and points added to determine a winner. Then the other clubs visited at Meadville. It was a family event where wives and children came also.

Three of his trophy buckles are still in the family's possession. One is labeled "1958 Meadville Champion Calf Roper" and the others are for steer roping.

ROPING CLUBS

I've been asked by lots of mugs
What ropers see in those roping clubs?
They chase those calves the live long day
Now how in hell do they get that way.

So read this through and I think you'll find
Just what goes on in a roper's mind.

Sunday early you come awake
For this is the day you've had to wait
You grain that horse and give him a rub
This is the day you rope that club.

Check your trailer and wonder when
That left hind tire will let go again
Load your horse and tie him good
Be sure he stands the way he should.

Start your trip with the kids all smiles
To those roping grounds about twenty miles.

Unload that horse and stack your gear
That roping match is drawing near
Check those ropes make sure they're right
The wind's come up and it's sure a fright.

Check the line-up and
    hear the worst
Not a friend in the
    world you're roping
    first
Get your number and
    there you see
They drew you out that
    number 3.

Jack on Roanie at the Meadville Roping Club

How does he run you
    always ask?
And finally find he's
    green as grass
If anyone knows they sure won't tell
You finally decide it's just as well.

So saddle your horse and set it tight
Those latigos must fit just right
Your second loop is shaped and hung
If you miss the first it must be swung.

Ride in the arena and move around
Let that old horse just feel the ground
Your stomach feels like a mess of snakes
You look at your hand and the damn thing shakes.

The announcer yells from the crow's nest roof
Your number three is in the chute
So you shake that loop if you have to wait
'Cause you sure don't want no figure eight.

Take one last look at your piggin' string
Remember the time you forgot the thing?
Ride in that box and your old horse knows
When he turns around away she goes.

The barrier's up the flag is too
The timer's ready and knows what to do
The field man sits in the field alone
As unconcerned as if he was home.

Everything's right and you can't wait
You nod your head and they open the gate
You nod your head so they can see
And out of the chute comes number 3.

You bail right out in that big old yard
My god I rode that barrier hard.
Can't spare 10 seconds in this old shop
But I didn't hear the damn thing pop.

Get him horse and give him hell
He's pulling right that just as well
Slide in close cause time's a thief
Stay with me lord let's pull in beef.

You die three times as your loop comes down
But she fits just right and you hit the ground
So sit down horse as I taught you to
And let me see what you can do.

Get down that rope and make it fast
Grab a leg and throw that calf.
Wrap him up and make it stay
'Cause you'll sure "no time" if he gets away.

Get up those hands, get off that calf
This must have taken an hour and a half
The flag man looks and damn his hide
For about an hour but the calf stays tied.

So you drag your rope and ride away
This must have been your lucky day
For the time says it's sure no dream
You got away in a flat fifteen.

So it goes from spring till fall
Heaven knows you can't catch them all
But you never know until you make your run
And after all it's just in fun.

But fall comes round and you sack your gear
You've just wound up another year
The one that's past don't mean a thing
And it's sure a hell of a long time till spring.

White Mare

ONE SPRING ALICE AND I went to a horse sale in Martin, S. D. We got there early and a horse dealer was trimming a little white mare in the ring. She was about the size of Alice's mare Princess and I thought I might buy her so we would have a pair of matched parade horses. They sold her green broke and I bought her. Didn't cost much as horses were pretty cheap that day.

When I got her under my saddle she was just like they said. Green broke but loved to kick. She was a little humpy so I didn't give her any excuse to buck. Didn't have time to really ride her so I sent her to Mullen to the Micheel boys to ride hell out of. They had her shaped up good and I was about to go after her.

Loyd Micheel likes mules and when he rented this ranch he ran all over putting some together. He had six or eight big good ones and was using them to stack and sweep hay with. The boys had the white mare at the hay field also.

It was coming up to rain hard with a lot of lightning. They unhooked the mules and as they were close to the buildings sent them to the barn on a lope. The rain and lightning hit as they finished unharnessing and the mules and white mare were in a tight bunch in the middle of the corral. The lightning hit them knocking them all down.

Micheel said the lightning and thunder jarred them in the barn but they sure thought all the mules were down and dead. One by one the mules picked up their heads, looked around, got up and walked away.

But not the white mare. She never moved so I suppose this goes to show mules are tougher than horses.

At least this time I have to agree.

COOKY

IDN'T OWN HER LONG, owned her longer than I should have and sure wasn't interested in owning her again.

She came through a horse sale in Valentine consigned by a horse dealer from North Platte. She was a ring reining fool. Not too pretty but put up to run and was sure sold that way. A fellow in Valentine had a granddaughter who needed a barrel horse. This mare's age was right and he bought her for the girl. I sort of needed a rope horse or a horse to make into one at the time and nearly bid on the mare at the sale.

He bought her for two hundred dollars which was a good enough buy. The next day the girl rode her and she never hesitated, just ran away. Of course, they decided to let her go. Actually the mare wasn't a runaway and had a good mouth. We found out later she had been raced quite a lot and just loved to run, and she was fast. I asked the man his price and as he was willing to settle for his purchase price, I took her and gave ten bucks to carry me till fall.

Rode her and she was real easy. Didn't care or even try to run her. Next spring decided I didn't need her so thought I might again sell her as a barrel horse but intended to work her a lot first as I didn't want to repeat the runaway.

One Sunday I saddled her just as a bunch of friends stopped by to visit. Of course this would have to take place with a corral full of people. I had told the truth about the mare admitting that I didn't know much about her. I soon found out how much I didn't know about her.

A fellow from South Dakota said he might use her and to step up and go around the barrels for him.

Now this mare had never given me any trouble. I don't really believe in tie downs on working horses and never had used one at all. I do believe in them on contest horses because that's a different deal. Those starts, stops,

156

and get downs are quick, sharp, and sudden and a loose tie down helps protect a rider's nose and teeth. For this reason I had stuck a cable noseband on this mare and decided later it was too tight. I think she lost her temper because of it and had told me in no uncertain terms.

Up until this time I had never been bucked off. I had been very, very lucky through the years. I'm sure I had sat out some pretty good storms but was a master at pulling leather, spurs in the cinch, yelling whoa, walking a ways or anything else to keep away from a bronc ride. At this time I was past riding broncs anyway but Cooky didn't take pity on me at all.

I just had a flat roping saddle on her with no spurs so she had the advantage of me but I doubt if it made much difference.

We went around the first barrel slow and easy, little faster to the second and when I let her out a little to the third I could feel her start to tighten up and get ready.

She gave me plenty of time to get ready.

I had a hand on the horn, reins solid in the other, both feet in the stirrups when she opened the show. She hit off to the left and sucked back, it felt pretty rough but I was still up and balanced. She hit to the right, sucked back and I thought, "Man, you're in a storm."

She hit to the left and she must have just been building a head of steam because when she sucked back that time they just played empty saddles.

The ground was soft, I hit sliding and wasn't hurt. The mare loped to the corral, I picked up my glasses and walked back.

I told them that was the first time for me and one guy said it sure as hell wasn't the first time for that mare. She could buck a little all right and I will always think it was because of the tie down being too tight.

I wouldn't sell her anywhere near home so hauled her to Council Bluffs to a horse sale where no one knew me. Though I didn't tell there that she was the only horse that ever threw me off, she didn't bring much money and I have stayed away from horse sales ever since.

How Man Got a Wife

Our modern stories tell us
Of the heights of true romance,
But when God created women
He didn't give the man a chance.

He gave the male no armor,
To defend him through his life,
He is bound to fall eventually
And get himself a wife.

They make us spend our
    money,
And we wonder how the
    heck,
We will live until next
    payday,
When we get another
check.

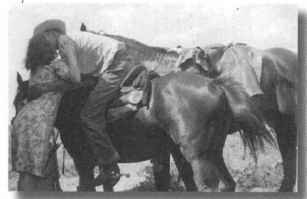

Jack kisses Alice good-bye

This goes on from month
to month,
And soon is very clear,
He is powerless to defend himself
When a woman is so near.

So he falls and is forgotten,
As he travels on life's path,
He wonders how it happened,
That he took a better half.

Then the stork got dingy,
And simply couldn't see
That one or two just wouldn't do,
So he up and sent him three!

God help that poor befuddled man,
As he travels through this life,
And help him try to understand,
Just how he got his wife.

He has a wife, three hearty boys,
Oh Gee, oh heck, of damn,
He sighs and seems to understand,
We have to live and learn.

Nobody's Home at Walter's

The morning I was driving by
I pulled into your yard
I yelled and screamed and stomped my feet
Then blew the horn real hard.

But no one came to welcome me
I really felt unwanted
So walked into your house to see
If the gosh darn thing was haunted.

I hoped to find a cook around
To hunt me up some dinner
But had to do the job myself
To keep from getting thinner.

I'm sure that you will never know
Who left this little mess
I'm not going to tell you
So you'll always have to guess.

So from the heart of every man
Who 'round the world does roam
I'm sure they say, "God Bless the Cook
Who sometimes stays at home.

1938 – Jack on Strip (Patty Ann's Mother)

Looking Around the Room at Walter's House

Look at all these little things
Gathered 'round our table
Maybe you can stand it
But we are hardly able.

Nicki sits and reads a book
She looks so awfully mean
Keevy does his very best
To be heard and also see.

Augie grunts and groans and moans
Messing with a top
While Ricki studies poems
He thinks will never stop.

Walter reads the paper
'Bout what we'll never know
Margaret simply can't decide
Which way she wants to go.

So as I look and listen
I only want to moan
Since I'm the nicest of the bunch
I guess I'll just go home.

Why Farmers Are Broke

A milk cow is a funny brute,
I know that you will laugh,
When I tell you of the places
They go to have a calf.

The first one picks a snow bank,
She heaves a mighty breath,
Then gets up and leaves it,
So it sure will freeze to death.

The second finds a swampy hole,
All nice and soft and cozy,
The calf he comes tumbling
And lands right on his snoozy.
P.S. He never gets up.

The third one hunts a big high cliff,
Now won't you stop and think,
The calf he comes but gosh ah gee,
He tumbles off the brink.

The fourth she lays down in the barn,
That's swell, but what the heck!!!
The calf bumps up against the wall,
And promptly breaks his neck.

A farmer's life is full of grief,
We cannot tell you half
Of the ways a cow can figure out,
To get rid of a calf.

The farmer tries with brain and pen,
To find some way to stop it,
But every spring he must admit,
"There goes my season's profit."

THE QUESTION IS "WHY?"

There's a millions of questions unanswered
Some are so blunt and some so sly
But the one that boggles our thinking
Is that everyone wants to know Why?

It starts when your mother conceives you
And looks at your Dad's twinkling eye
She's happy of course that you happened
But I'm sure that she's wondering Why?

So now that the question is final
And you hit the world on the fly
You'll think for sure, for the rest of your life
That everyone wants to know Why?

Why'd you do this, Why'd you do that
Why didn't you tell a white lie
You think conversation is made up of words
All ending with one question Why?

Since Adam and Eve ate the apple
And were kicked from the garden on high
That old serpent just sat there and chuckled
And Adam and Eve wondered Why?

So sure are our own death and taxes
I'll bet lots of bucks when I die
The question will still be unanswered
Why everyone wants to know Why?

Can You Explain?

Can anybody tell me?
Why a dog will chase a cat?
Why we all get our directions mixed.
And don't know where we're at.
Why the rooster crows at daybreak.
Why the owls fly 'round at night.
Why trout swim up the highest falls.
And why two brothers fight

Have you ever stopped and wondered,
Why the world is made so round,
Why the stars come out at evening
And the sky is not the ground
Why the moon comes up and sun goes down
In every kind of weather.
Yet in all the years they've traveled
They have never bumped together

Why are some folks always fat,
No matter how they diet
And skinny folks just can't get fat,
'Cause I have seen them try it.
Why do coyotes howl at a new full moon,
Why do canaries sing,
Why do leaves fall off in winter.
And grass comes up in spring.

I have often tried to understand
Why left is never right.
Why a cat will light upon its feet,
And day is never night.
Why a squirrel will run around a tree,
Why white is never black,
And when you are going forward,
You are never coming back.

Why do rabbits act so timid,
Why does every bed bug bite,
Why do hens all roost at evening,
And not lay eggs at night.
These questions have me dizzy,
My mind is very hazy.
So now I think I'd better stop,
Before we both go crazy.

A 25TH Anniversary

Written for Alice's sister Margaret Fox and husband Wes on their 25th anniversary

Here's to the dears who've been married 5 years
And here's to the ones married 10
I'm sure there are plenty
Who've been married twenty
And managed this much with good cheer.

But those who survive and make 25
Have lived with each other quite steady
It isn't the time that has passed on behind
It's the time it takes to get ready.

Now here is the way for many a day
They work all their friends and neighbors
As Sunday draws nigh with time passing by
You wish for a whole delegation.

Plant the garden, paint the fences
Lay the rugs down on the floor
Clean the yard and burn the trash up
Put some varnish on the door

Paint the woodwork hang the curtains
Clean the pictures on the wall
Fix the windmills fix the fences
Sweep the floors out in the hall

Paint the screens and clean the car out
Get the washing on the line
Go to town and get some groceries
'Cause we're running out of time.

Clean the bathrooms check the cattle
Now be sure you do it right
Make some coffee wash the dishes
'Cause by now it's Saturday night.

So there are the ways that we've spent our days
Just getting all ready for Sunday
But these ladies and lads will be awfully glad
When they wake up and find out it's Monday.

So please as you stay at Fox's this day
Enjoying the things that have filled us
Be glad man alive it was just 25
'Cause 50 would surely have killed us.

A Thought

Sun is setting, Evening's coming,
Sky is red and gold
Cowbells tinkling, wind is sighing,
This is ours to hold.

Milk pails rattle, insects humming,
Never from afar,
Here we live, here we're contented.
No crime our joy to man.

Supper over, work is finished,
It's so wonderful to live,
Never scheming nor surprising,
Just to be and love and give.

Here's our home, it's what we make it,
Joy and peace, my home to stay,
Now how could we be unhappy
When God's blessed us day by day.

Wash Day

The house is torn up
The kids are a mess
I know what's the matter
I don't have to guess.
No dinner to eat
As a matter of course
Nothing else matters
The girls have to wash.

They hunt up the soap
The boilers and tubs
Heat up some water
Get ready to scrub.
Then get out of the way
Don't draw a long breath
If you're in the way
You'll get trampled to death.

Don't bother them now
There's some on the line
More of them coming
And everything's fine.
Then the wash machine stops
Cause it runs out of gas
These dames get so mad
They roll in the grass.

Then everything's fixed
Till the wringer won't ring
Then Daddy must come
And fix the damn thing.
The clothes line falls down
Before they are through
And Daddy must come and fix that up to.

The clothes are all dry
But it's Daddy's chore
To pack out the tubs
Cause they leak on the floor.
And bring the clothes
And throw out the starch
Cause everyone's washing
And daddy must march.

Now everything's finished
It wasn't much fun
The girls heave a sigh
Just see what *we've* done.
But Daddy goes on to finish his work
Cause everyone's washing
And he mustn't shirk.

So on wash day beware
Of our home on the creek
Cause there's nothing to wear
And nothing to eat.
But if you insist and don't give a damn
Remember it's wash day
The mud hits the fan.

LETTER TO HELEN DREWS
about Ray Bennett's Story Ponca, Nebr.

DEAR HELEN,

I have a little story that I don't think should be lost. Even though I came to Ponca in 1971 to wrangle horses for the state of Nebraska, we take the home paper and I'm always interested in the old stories and pictures that are mentioned. As we know, if old facts are not pictured or written or verified in some way they are lost and it is a loss that can never be regained.

I thought in some way with your work with the historical society you might be interested in this one. Even though my ancestors came to Cherry County between 1879 and 1882 this story does not concern them.

This was told to me in Erlyn McCray's barber shop by Ray Bennett there in town. Of course the story is as my memory says, but Ray can sure pickup the facts. It seems Ray's family, parents and some grandparents came out of Kansas with their household goods in wagons and trailing whatever livestock they owned. Ray said he was pretty small but big enough to ride and keep the livestock moving.

They settled on the Snake River, more or less south of Cody in that Barnes country.

One morning all of the older men left home early to get to Cody. During the afternoon Ray's mother was bitten on the leg by a rattle snake. She did the usual such as lancing the fang marks and putting a fresh killed chicken for a poultice. She sent Ray to the neighbors for help. The lady who was there had a baby and for transportation an old grey mare and a mule colt.

Of course she went back to Bennett's with Ray. And it was nearly dark when they got home. Apparently some one along the way had a telephone so they called a doctor and left word in Cody for the men.

As it happened, as it was nearly dark, they put Ray's little sister on the horse with him to go get the milk cows. Ray said the darkest summer storm came up you ever saw. One of those kinds – that curl your hair from

173

lightning and the thunder makes you deaf. Ray said when the storm was over, you couldn't see anything and wet and cold as they were he just turned the old mare loose and let her take them home with no milk cows.

Now came the problem. The neighbor's baby was fed on a bottle and the milk supply was gone. After trying everything such as sugar and water, etc., the baby was still very, very unhappy. The neighbor lady took a small bucket and left the house for a few minutes and when she came back she had a couple of cups of milk.

Ray said it took awhile to figure out where she got it but he sure remembers the baby drank the milk, went to sleep and never said a word till morning and he was sure of that because they were up all night caring for his mother.

Sometime the next afternoon the family from Cody and the doctor (I don't recall the name) got back to the ranch and the doctor took over from there and the mother got along O.K. The doctor had come to Cody on the train and on to the ranch on horseback.

To me this is so much human interest here and how little we realize how much has been accomplished in that area in a realistically short time. From the time of this story till now is less than 70 years.

I'm afraid not many mothers would know how to steal milk from a mule colt. How many doctors would go by train to Cody and on to the Snake horse back? How many little kids are caught in a rain storm jingling milk cows?

Hell, Helen – someone else can have the good old days. I'll take mine, now.

Yours,

Jack Galloway

P.S. This can be checked with Ray Bennett there in town if anyone has use for it.

Wisdom from Jack's Letters

Jack in 1982

JACK BECAME A PROLIFIC letter writer as he was tethered to an oxygen tank because of asthma, allergies and emphysema. Some of his letters were sad as he related being lonesome but some were funny as he looked at life and tried to figure out people. Included is a small sampling of those letters, most without a true date, just the day and time.

Here is an excerpt from a letter he sent from Jack's Tack Shop dated

"Tues. – 10:30 Tack Shop." My oxygen man is supposed to be in this afternoon so that will break the day up some. I only stay open until 5. Right now I feel anyone who wants in here will either come or want something bad enough to call.

I did order about 200 bucks worth of riding tack. It should come today but haven't seen them yet. I just stay with my Perkies outfit (his supply catalog) up in Minn. Their stuff is just plain old gear but year after year their quality stays the same.

We tried other outfits last year and they call about every week but I can't get along with their gear.

I tell everybody they have to be satisfied after they walk out my door and if I never make a dine I intend to keep that a fact.

Tuesday evening 5:00 12th

The weather has turned to winter. Not really cold but just stays cloudy and rains and snows and freezes on everything. The temperature just stays between 24 and 35 degrees. I get a little lonesome when I'm stuck here all day but I'm getting a little more adjusted to it. Isn't quite as bad as it used to be, so will try to let "Mind over Matter" take over. Can fill up mornings pretty well with cooking, exercises, shaving, etc. The evenings are O.K. with television, but afternoons get pretty long because I can't get interested in those damn Soap Operas.

The sale days worked out pretty well. Made a little money and some new customers. Also a couple of people who are paying on their saddles stopped in with their payments so I was satisfied.

Ponca will have a new look at least on one corner in the near future. The lumber yard went out of business and a guy has been junking out the lumber. I guess everyone in town except me had already found out that a new Post Office is to be built there. Guess the government isn't broke. Suppose they would like a Tack Shop to finish the project?

You better take good care of your Johnny horse. A person only gets 1 or 2 of those in a lifetime. Horses like Old Buck get good because they are all you have and they just do everything because you and they have to. That's kind of the way Lucky was. We didn't ever really have one like that. All my horses were rodeod or raced and even though they were gentle weren't nice for kids or scared girls. Horses you can trust just aren't to be found any more.

1:30 afternoon the next day

Think I'll put on a little stew as I notice about 6 things that need used up. Celery, etc. That's the nice thing about stew. You put in everything you don't need any more and dump it out if it isn't any good. You haven't lost a thing. P.S. It was pretty good.

Ponca – Mon. morning

I'm sending an "I'm Alive" note. This weather is goofy. Today is to start hot and drop to 70 this afternoon. Now that's odd. I'm O.K. Am real careful. The lilacs are down a little and the spirea is still bad. Now I notice the brome grass is going into pollen stage. I feel O.K., eat pretty well and breath as well as I can expect. If anything isn't O.K., I'll call.

Another day at 2:00.

Ate lunch – took a snooze. Nothing new so will finish this and go to the P.O. and on with my afternoon of doing nothing.

Ponca Mon. 9:20

Have had a few pretty fair days at the shop. Nothing great but enough to let me pay my past due insurance on the shop. Must get a small order sent. Had a run on cinches and ran plumb out. Also need buckles and a couple of blankets.

Sunday is really a lost day in Ponca. I was at the shop and felt like I was getting claustrophobic or something. Just said nuts about 2:30 and locked up. Drove around down town. The only thing I saw alive was Henry Riffey sitting on his porch. He was asleep so I wasn't so sure about him. Both bars were closed and both filling stations. I think one store and the ice cream place were open but no one near them.

Drove up to Newcastle and watched a couple of innings of baseball. Went south to Martinsburg. Came to the west end of Main Street and couldn't get out to the highway. Thought there must have been a shooting or something with so many cars. Asked a couple of gals the score and it was a tractor pull. I knew those were popular but didn't expect that big a crowd in Martinsburg for anything. Finally worked my way around the big city and out to the road.

Have had the T.V. on this morning. Discovered I'm away behind on my quiz shows. Guess I'll just look on this day as a vacation I don't need and enjoy it.

Still haven't made the barber shop. As you know I sure did and still do

177

need to. First cool day I'll get it done. Hair is so long can't even anchor my hat.

Sunday 12:30 1986

Got some new tablets and I really like them because I can get a lot of words on a sheet.

Have had quite a few visitors (at his shop) since I have been here. Haven't sold an awful lot but all of the time hasn't been wasted. Have sold the pony harness, saddle blanket, spur straps, 3 pr. Reins, 1 rope, cinch cover, and cinch. About 150 bucks or so. Got the shipment of gear from Minn. Didn't make too big a pile, $175 or so. Trouble was some of the spurs and reins I wanted I have to reorder. Sold a bull whip 12 ft. to a gal. She is a little slow and I'm real careful to not sell her anything out of reason. She is a darn good customer and they have money. Just shells out the cash. I was a little doubtful about the whip but when I quizzed her I sure found out she has one old cow when she has a calf wants to fight her horse. She just bets when she gets that 12 ft. whip the cow will behave. I sold her an 8 ft. one a couple of years ago. She only has one horse but enough equipment for 3. Wish I had more slow customers like her.

Sure isn't much if any corn up around here. It was just too wet and cold. Seems like all of the ground you can see is upside down so they are really at it now.

A fellow gave me a nice present at the shop. He has sprayed the neighbors and me for dandelions and we just don't have any. Costs $15 a year but it has weed killer and fertilizer in it. Really works. He asked if I wanted sprayed at the shop and I told him it was sure O.K. if he could get them on each side to go along. They wouldn't go along so in the evening he had some spray left so he did mine for free. He even said thanks to me for letting him do it. Said he was going to make the neighbors ashamed. It's one time something is on my side so I'll just set back and giggle.

Called the pop company this morning, so maybe we'll get that machine taken care of and settle down for a summer season. If my shop is a sample, I don't want a department store!

Becky

Waiting for Becky's Baby

I have a sweet Granddaughter
And she's really on the level
It's a good thing she got married
"Cause she's full of little devils.

She up and had us two good boys
And though it ain't no fun
She's going down the same darn route
To have another one.

She keeps procrastinating
And fooling with the date
But I have finally figured out
The reason she's so late.

They can't tell what to name it
Although they've gone and looked
All through the family bible
And all the history books.

They try the names on for a boy
They try them for a girl
So Grand Dad Jack laid down the law
Now give this one a whirl.

Just try on all the names you find
Like Maynard, Paul, and Harley
But when this baby GIRL is born
We're going to call her CHARLIE.

Now Charlie's tired of waiting
And so am I in fact.
So find a good delivery room
That's orders
Grand Dad Jack

(Jack didn't get Charlie. Becky delivered another boy!)

Becky was Jack's first grandchild and only girl. He thought she was the absolute best grandchild. He taught her some of her first words, including "Damn dog," and he taught her to eat radishes and blue cheese dressing on salads when she was about 17 months old.

My Granddad Jack

He was born in the Sandhills
A hundred years too late
For the life he wanted to lead
Jack was a different breed.

He spoke of days no more
Of the ranch and the cowboys
Of earning a living from the ground
Of the days when a horse was the way to town.

He was tall and lanky
With hair of black
That thinned and grayed
After Gram went on her way.

But from him I learned
A lot of the rules of life
How to laugh, how to cry
How to keep on giving living a try.

From the time I was born
He's a constant in my memory
And if I could, I'd turn the clock back
And look once more at the face of my Granddad Jack.

Becky Roanne Hamar, 1989

1962 – Jack with his first grandchild, Becky Hamar

HOME

When it's evening on the prairie,
And the sun has gone to rest,
Behind the tumbling sandhills.
Rolling far into the west.
See the summer swallows flitting,
Hither thither in the sky,
Hear the cowbells gently tinkling
And the night wind's gentle sigh.

The tiny stars came blinking
From their nest in hazy blue,
Like the eyes of little animals,
When everything is new.
Then the yellow moon comes smiling
And our very being thrills.
While the northern lights climb higher,
Along the northern hills.

We hear Coalie's gentle nicker,
From his pasture by the mill,
Then a stallion's ringing challenge.
From the rimrock on the hills.
In the distance comes the lowing,
Of the cattle by the lake
Then the coyote's weird yodel
Then the answer from its mate.

You can have your lighted cities,
We'll admit they're mighty fine,
But I'll take a horse and saddle,
And a quiet range for mine.
Where the sandhills roll forever,
And that endless prairie land,
Where nature takes the weakling,
And every man's a man.

Always Coming Home
to the Sandhills

PROBABLY IT'S ONLY NATURAL for a person to think the locality in which they were raised and grew to manhood is the greatest on earth. To be sure many boys are seized with the so called "itchy foot" and ramble over considerable chunks of country before they settle down. It has been my observation that they generally return to their home communities when their toes have been scratched enough, or possibly, too much for comfort.

The Sandhills and Cherry County is a pretty big piece of ground in itself. Many boys grow up and eventually own ranches without getting beyond the broad reaches of the Sandhills and more than you would probably think never travel beyond the state boundaries. Why? Simply because the Sandhills are an education in themselves and a person has nearly a complete education by the time he masters them.

So is it any wonder the boys jerked from our communities and thrown into training centers in the east suffer from homesickness? In their past experience any place at meal time or bedtime was a home to them. To be sure these places may have been 20 long miles apart but if it had an empty saddle peg and feed for a hungry fuzzy tail it was home to any cowboy drifting by.

Come morning and a heartfelt "thank you" and it was the long trail ahead, but always with the assurance of a happy welcome at whatever outfit he may hit at sundown.

Now in the east the houses are close together, the farms small and unnatural. The people in a hurry and apparently unfriendly. This needless to say makes our boys realize how far from home they really are.

But most of all the boys miss the open country. This I can readily understand as my one trip of any distance, a mere 300 miles into eastern

Nebraska made me realize how big our Sandhills really were. This was at State Fair time and many 4-H boys and girls of my own age. Of course we were interested in where everyone else lived. Invariably the question arose, "How big is your farm?" Some of these fellows would hang their heads and sheepishly admit, "40 acres." Others in reply to the same question would threaten to pop buttons off their shirts when they replied, "A big one, 180 acres."

Needless to say it seemed queer to me when I knew that our outfit -5000 odd acres -wouldn't make a bump in some of the pastures of the Sandhills.

I stood it for three days and was about as homesick a kid as ever left Cherry County. Never before or since has the sight of those rolling plains, hills and cattle looked so good to me as they did that evening as we hit the Sandhills at sundown doing a prewar 60 miles per hour. And to this day I have had no inclination to leave at any time.

Perhaps this will help you understand why a boy can be plenty lonesome and blue though he may be among thousands of people and plenty of money in his pocket.

Ask him what he would like most and I'll bet he tells you, my horse, my saddle, and enough Sandhills to spend 8 hours on the horse and saddle and see nothing but cactus, coyotes, cattle, and more Sandhills.

SANDHILL BURIAL

He was a cowboy, the last of his breed,
And she was his lady to fill every need.

I was their child, rode a horse before talking,
Aboard a four legged animal before I was walking.

Through the years I left them, and moved far away,
I saved all their letters, I read them today.

I was called back, after they had both died,
Picked a spot at the graveyard near her folks, and I cried.

They're back in the Sandhills where they needed to be,
They wanted buried where they once rode free.

They are laid to rest where the pine trees sway,
Where sand swirls around them on each windy day.

They're together and happy, I like to believe,
Then I walk away, I leave them, and grieve.

He was a cowboy, the last of his breed,
And she was his lady to fill every need.

Nancy Galloway Hamar

Glossary

There are words used in this book that some readers might not know. Many of them are not found in any dictionary. The people referred to have also been identified and the different landmarks Jack talks about along the Niobrara River.

Alice (Manifold) Galloway: Jack's wife from 1937 until her death in 1985.

Balk: When a horse stops, refusing to go forward.

Barrier: In a rodeo roping event, a light rope is stretched in front of the chute holding a calf or steer. The horse should not touch the barrier before the critter releases it automatically or the roper will be penalized 10 seconds.

Caking cattle: A term used for feeding range cubes or cotton cake to beef cows out on pasture. They are grain cubes about the size of a fun size Snickers and are an efficient way to get food to cattle as a supplement to the grass hay stacked for them during the summer. Jack carried cake to his cows in gunny sacks tied to the saddle horn and strung out on the ground when he got to the cows.

Car crossing: Sometimes referred to as an "auto gate," it is a series of pipes laid over a pit and secured in cement. Cattle or horses will not walk over it but a vehicle can safely cross. It took the place of gates that had to be opened by hand. Of course, the original gates were left in place to use when horseback riding, driving a team or moving cattle.

Cold jawed: When a horse does not respond to a bridle bit in its mouth and no amount of pulling or jerking will make him pay attention.

Dad: This is Andrew Jackson Galloway, Jack's father. He is married to Jennie and they are the parents of Jack, Don, Jim, and Beth.

Dally: A wrap around the saddle horn taken after a critter is roped.

Forest reserve: A large area of range owned by the federal government and leased to ranchers to make hay or to graze cattle or horses. Today it is called the McKelvie National Forest.

Gay: During the 1930s, gay meant happy, having a fun time.

Granddad: James Thomas "Jim" Galloway, Jack's paternal grandfather. He was a homesteader/rancher after marrying Agnes Roberts and then became a stone mason in Valentine. He built many of the cement block buildings still standing on Main Street.

Horse names: The Johnny and Old Buck referred to in a letter were horses owned by Nancy Galloway Hamar's family. Lucky was a sorrel horse Nancy started riding at age three and Lucky was three also.

Jingle pasture: A small pasture where a horse is kept overnight to use to bring in the horses for the day's work or to gather the milk cows. To "jingle" the horses is to go after them.

Latigo: A piece of leather on a saddle that is used on the left side to fasten to the cinch and used to tighten the saddle on a horse. A short latigo is on the right side and it stays solid and is not changed each time the horse is saddled.

Lope: A horse's gait faster than a trot, usually a gentle forward movement the dude's call a "gallop."

Loop: A circle in the rope that is thrown over a critter's head. A loop aimed for a cow is shaped differently than one used to rope horses.

Old ranch: This piece of land was owned by J.T. Galloway and later sold. When Jack refers to the "old ranch," that is the place he tells about.

"Pup" hole: This refers to a prairie dog hole, which could be lethal to a horse if it was running and stepped into one. Badger holes were also dangerous to horses.

Rauer place: This land was west of A.J. Galloway's place nestled along the

Niobrara River and home to Jack and Alice after their marriage. An old German named Julius Rauer owned it previously and when Alice washed the cabin windows, Julius thought they had installed new ones.

Throw rope: What dudes might call a "lasso." Jack always referred to this tool as a "throw rope," even after he started roping calves and steers in rodeos.

Walter: Was Walter Galloway, Jack's cousin who lived east "down" the river. Ted is another cousin but he lived "up" the river to the west.

ABOUT THE AUTHOR

THE ACTUAL AUTHOR OF most of these stories is Jack Junior Galloway, born in the Sandhills of Nebraska in 1919 and died in those same Sandhills in 1987, but the person responsible for this compilation of his letters, poems and stories is his oldest daughter, Nancy Jo Galloway Hamar.

Nancy Galloway Hamar married young – 18 – and left the Sandhills when her husband, Roland "Smokey" Hamar, made the decision to farm instead of ranch. They bought a small farm in Southern Iowa, expanded to a few more acres when it became available and then moved "to town" – Allerton, Iowa, Population 539 in the mid-1980's. It was during this time that Nancy's oldest son, Bob, was working for the weekly newspaper in Corydon, IA., and he told her that the publisher was looking for someone to help out with covering the Wayne County Fair. She took on the challenge and never looked back. She wrote a weekly column for that newspaper for over 20 years, she covered school boards and fair boards and city councils, met and wrote about interesting people every week and never ever stopped learning. She buried her mother, her father, her grandmother, her husband, her son Dave and she never stopped writing, and she never stopped learning.

A tradition in Nancy's family – her children, grandchildren and great-grandchildren – is whenever and wherever they celebrate Christmas, at the end of the evening wine is poured and toast is drank "To those who came before us and to those who will come after us". This book is dedicated to her father and those that came after him, but this book is really about a daughter's love for her daddy and making sure that what he wrote so long ago is preserved for the generations to come.